From the Pulpit

of

Saint James School

COLLECTED THOUGHTS
OF A PRIEST HEADMASTER

D. Stuart Dunnan

Published by
Watson Publishing International
for

Saint James School
2002

First published in the United States of America
by Watson Publishing International
Post Office Box 493
Canton, MA 02021-0493

Library of Congress Cataloging-in-Publication Data
Dunnan, D. Stuart, 1959–
    From the pulpit of Saint James School : collected thoughts of a priest
    headmaster / D. Stuart Dunnan.
        p.   cm.
    Includes bibliographical references.
    ISBN 0-88135-370-1 (pbk.)
    1. Saint James School (Hagerstown, Md.)   2. Dunnan, D. Stuart, 1959–
    3. Episcopal Church—Education.   I. Saint James School (Hagerstown, Md.)
    II. Title.
    LD7501.H17 D86 2002
    371.071'83—dc21
                                                            2002033195
ISBN 0-88135-370-1

Designed and typeset by Publishers' Design and Production Services, Inc.
Manufactured in the USA.

PREFACE

HE FOLLOWING COLLECTION OF SERMONS, essays and occasional letters has been assembled at the suggestion of Neale Watson to mark my first ten years as Headmaster of Saint James School. Neale's brother Albert taught English at Saint James for many years with great distinction, and I first met Neale prior to presiding at Albert's burial, and then again at their father's burial, sadly in the same year. Neale's enthusiasm for Saint James School and his strong support for me personally as a priest cannot go unacknowledged, and so, I wish particularly to thank him.

In discussing this collection, it was Neale's suggestion that we arrange the material chronologically, rather than by genre or by theme. In this way, readers familiar with independent schools can discern the progress of Saint James over the last decade, as well as my own growth as headmaster. Similarly, those familiar with the priesthood and those familiar with the role of a priest headmaster in Episcopal schools in particular will discern, I hope, the development of my own theology in the work I have enjoyed here, and the deepening of my own vocation. Finally, those familiar with boarding schools will appreciate, I think, the new apology for boarding which we have developed here in response to the changing culture of America around us, specifically our commitment to community as essential to the moral and spiritual growth of teenagers and our belief in the strong relationships between students and between teachers and students which real community sustains.

For those unfamiliar with Saint James, we begin with the school's philosophy, which I wrote for our Middle States evaluation three years ago. I hope this will give you some sense of the place and some sense of me, as you enter into the story which follows. In many ways, Saint James is unique: we are smaller and more traditional than other college preparatory schools, and probably more of a church, certainly more of a Catholic school than other Episcopal institutions, because of our Tractarian foundation and our faithfulness to it. Nonetheless, we are still a school like other schools, full of teenagers learning in classrooms, playing on teams, acting in plays, and pretending to sleep in the dormitories; we just pray in Chapel. Like all good schools, we are committed to the moral and spiritual development of our students, and therefore find ourselves to some extent at war with the self-centered and self-serving culture of fame and wealth around us. Therefore, I am hopeful that others will find in my words their own schools and their own challenges, because most of these we share.

Before concluding, let me also thank Admiral James L. Holloway, III, Jeremy Biggs, and the other trustees who appointed a 33-year-old academic from Oxford with a fake English accent, and have supported me generously, and really quite bravely, ever since. Let me thank Chick Meehan, Sandra Pollock, and Marty Collin who greeted me so generously when I arrived, and all the excellent administrators, faculty, and staff who have worked so hard to make me look good, especially my excellent assistant Ellen Davis and Erin Harman in the Development Office who helped gather the material for this collection. But let me especially thank the students of Saint James who have supported me with a remarkable devotion, who have taught me so much about life, about courage, growth and grace, and who have helped me to build this wonderful school. They are the soul of Saint James and the joy of my ministry. Without them and without the pleasure of their company, my work would become a job.

Finally, I dedicate this book to my parents, Diana and Weaver Dunnan, who have always been generous and kind to me, and who have loved me as myself, even so much that they let me be myself. In truth, they did not just send me to school like their other children; they gave me to school, and they never got me back.

The Revd. Dr. D. Stuart Dunnan,
A.B., A.M., (Harvard); M.A., D.Phil., (Oxford)
Saint James School
April 2002

PHILOSOPHY

OUNDED IN 1842 by the leaders of the Oxford Movement in the Episcopal Church, Saint James School remains faithful to our historic identity as a Church School, maintaining the spiritual witness and discipline of regular corporate Anglican worship, and continuing our attention to the spiritual and moral formation of our students. As an Episcopal school, Saint James welcomes students and faculty of all faiths, supporting each in our common pilgrimage of life.

Believing that young people are raised best in close relationship with each other and with adults who care for them, we remain committed to our enduring character as a small, coeducational boarding school with a limited number of day students predominately in the younger forms. In educating our students, we seek to develop and nurture all their talents and intelligences, challenging them to grow academically, athletically, artistically, socially, and morally in the context of a close and supportive residential community.

To this end, we offer a substantial and appropriate college preparatory program in small classes maintained by a low student-to-teacher ratio. We require a rigorous core curriculum in English, math, science, history, and language, with additional electives in each discipline. We require full participation in athletics and offer a broad program for interscholastic competition in three seasons, which emphasizes team participation and individual athletic development. We also require participation in the arts, offering opportunities for academic study in art and music, as well as opportunities for extracurricular participation and performance in drama, visual art, and instrumental and choral music.

Faculty at Saint James are expected to care for their students and to teach for their success. Students at Saint James are expected to treat each other and their teachers with respect, to assume responsibility for their own actions, to follow the honor code, and to obey the school's rules. These rules are designed to preserve the character and decorum of the school as a society for learning and to protect the safety and dignity of each individual member.

Every student is expected to set the right example as a member of our society and to contribute to the community of the school. As students grow older, they are called to positions of responsibility and leadership in their various activities and in the residential life of the school. These positions are intended to challenge and develop these students as leaders for good and to empower them to serve and help their fellow students.

By maintaining a school which is both traditional and tolerant, small and diverse, we hope to establish in microcosm our vision for a better society at large. By challenging our students to lead for good within our community, we hope to prepare them to lead for good in the world. By requiring all our students to serve others outside the school even while they are with us, we seek to remind them of the greater opportunities for service which await them as occasions for grace and fulfillment in their lives.

A Sermon
On the Occasion
of the 150th Anniversary
# of Saint James School

O N THE 9TH OF MARCH, 1841, the distinguished churchman and educator, William Augustus Muhlenberg wrote to Bishop Whittingham of Maryland regarding the Bishop's new project of founding a diocesan school. The Bishop had originally written to Muhlenberg in the hope that he could lure him away from the school which he had founded (Saint Paul's School at College Point in New York) to the Bishop's new school at Fountain Rock in Maryland, tentatively named "Saint James Hall." Saint Paul's was, in fact, the first Episcopal boarding school ever to be founded on the English model in the United States; Saint James was to be the second. Muhlenberg had decided that he could not go himself, so he proposed to send his closest and most intimate disciple, his "second in command" at College Point, the Revd. Dr. John Barrett Kerfoot. Commending Kerfoot to Bishop Whittingham, Muhlenberg writes of his dream for the Bishop's new school:

Right Revd. and Dear Sir,—The more I think of the proposed branch of our institution in your diocese, the more disposed I feel to attempt to realize it.

I believe it would operate favorably on the cause of education in various ways, and not the least by showing the true way of beginning a Church School. I have often wished for an opportunity of starting de novo, *with a few select men and with perfect independence as to patronage. This, it appears to me, we could do at "Fountain Rock." We would send out a colony of pious, intelligent, respectable young fellows, with Kerfoot at their head, who would care nothing about their support, and enter upon their work* con *amore. They would be the soul of the thing and gradually they would gen-erate the body around them.*[1]

And so, on this day when we remember that "colony of pious, intelligent, respectable young fellows" and give thanks to God for the school which they started, let us take the words of Muhlenberg as our text: "They would be the soul of the thing and gradually they would generate the body around them."

And this is a good text for us, I think, because it reminds us that this school is at heart a community, a community of scholars: teachers and students. For it was this belief in community which inspired Dr. Muhlenberg to found his school in the first place. Christians, who believe that God is love, believe in the community of love. We believe that human beings are called to live together in peace, in mutual respect, and in mutual affection. And so, by founding a Christian school, Muhlenberg hoped to establish a strong community of scholars which would not only teach students knowledge, but also teach human beings how to love each other, how to live and work together for the greater development of each individual's gifts and thus for the greater good of all.

This was Muhlenberg's "beau ideal" of a "Catholic School," a "genuine Church School," as he put it, "something of a kind which ha[d] not been realized in this part of the world."[2] The whole ideal for Saint James was perhaps best expressed by our co-founder, The Revd. Dr. Theodore Lyman, then Rector of Saint John's, Hagerstown. In his view, Saint James should be:

> . . . *a school religiously guided and controlled as a Church family and Church congregation, ordered and taught as such, in all points of duty, truth and worship: the life of religion made, by God's grace, to vivify the academ-ical family; the minister of the Church being at once the father and pastor of the household and congregation; not a system of ecclesiastical routine and theological lectures but, by the grace of the Holy Spirit, the honest, practical life of faith energizing the whole body and seeking the sanctification of all of its members.*[3]

---

[1] H. Harrison, *Life of Kerfoot* (New York, 1886), vol. i, p. 33.
[2] Harrison, i, p. 34.
[3] As quoted in *Saint James School: 125th Anniversary*, p. 5.

And it is remarkable how faithful the school has remained to this vision. We remain at our core a community at prayer. Every weekday begins with Chapel, every formal meal begins with grace. And as we gather in this place and in the dining room, we experience every day anew what it means not just to work together, but to live together, not just to recognize each other, but to know each other, not just to accept each other, but to help each other.

And it is this essential aspect of our character, this, our overriding commitment to being a community, which sets this school apart from other schools. Students do not just go to Saint James; they belong to Saint James: they belong to a family, a family of scholars certainly, but more than this, a family of friends.

And so, as I prepared for this sermon and attempted some reading on the history of the school, Muhlenberg's Letter to Bishop Whittingham provided the most appropriate text: "they would be the soul of the thing and gradually they would generate the body around them;" for it was with that first group of young scholars gathered around Dr. Kerfoot that this school took root. And it was their dedication, their common devotion to the demanding and challenging task of teaching and raising young people in an atmosphere of mutual love and respect which raised this school as a beacon of faith upon this hill.

And over these one hundred and fifty years, many have come here, now girls as well as boys, day students as well as boarders. And all of them have come here drawn by the same light, the light first raised by Kerfoot and his followers and kept burning here ever since; burning in times of war and times of peace, burning in times of want and times of plenty. And through it all, the young have come here, here to be taught, here to be encouraged, directed, and set free, free to make the world a better place, free to bring the kingdom they have prayed for here closer to our world.

And so, my sermon is not so much a sermon to those who have gone before and still remember us with affection, or even those who would help us now. It is to us, to those of us who are here now, those of us who work and live here on this hill together, those of us who are called to this place to keep the light of faith alive: faith in God, faith in His truth and His goodness, and His beauty; and faith in our calling to follow in His way of love, to follow after Christ towards that truth, that goodness, and that beauty which Christ Himself has revealed to us.

But even here, I cannot just look around me; I must look, in the end, to myself. For by some remarkable act of grace, I find myself standing in this pulpit as Dr. Kerfoot's most unworthy successor. And, as I face the challenges of the present moment, I am humbled by the achievements of those who have gone before me. Kerfoot founded this School in 1842 only to lose everything he had worked for in the insanity of the Civil War, but the words of his final address to the College of Saint James on the 9th of July in 1862 still remind us of his faith and of his courage:

> *It is our hope and resolve to keep our College alive, and busy in so much of this work as God may now send it; and ready for full work when He shall restore to us the usual scope and demand for it. To-day we choose not to measure our College by the mere present. We think of the seven hundred and twelve pupils who, through twenty years, have been under our tuition. And we remember, too, how often the hours and the youths that seemed to promise no fruit in requital for our efforts, have turned out before our own eyes the most fruitful hours and hearts in our record. So do we care the less to-day that the times have left us but three graduates, when we know that these make up the fair, satisfying sum of ninety-one graduates at fifteen commencements. We expect to send out many more good men such as we now know among the hundreds who have been here. But, even if this were not our hope now, none of us would deem the past a vain expenditure of time and work for any of us.*
>
> *Other Christian Colleges, preceptors and pupils will grow out of this work here. The foundations are laid deep and sure. The walls have risen up high enough to develop the work and tell of its full outline and sober dignity. Future years and other men must and shall take up the task and complete it.*[4]

And Kerfoot's words, of course, were indeed prophetic, for his college survives to this day as Saint James School. And from his college have sprung other schools, each also faithful to his vision: Kerfoot's disciple, the Revd. Dr. Henry Augustus Coit left Saint James to serve as the first rector of Saint Paul's School in Concord, New Hampshire; Kerfoot's nephew, former student, and former tutor in the college, the Revd. John Kerfoot Lewis went off to serve as the first headmaster of Saint Mark's School in Southborough,

---

[4] Harrison, i, pp. 230–231.

Massachusetts; and it was the example of Saint Mark's which inspired the Revd. Endicott Peabody to found Groton School as well.[5] And now, because Muhlenberg's own school did not long survive the founding of this one, Saint James stands proud as the oldest Episcopal school modeled on Muhlenberg's original vision.

And there is a reason why we have survived so long: Kerfoot has had several worthy successors. Henry Onderdonk came to this school in 1869 and rebuilt it after the Civil War. His son, Adrian, came in 1903 and restored the school after a period of decline. In this, he was beset with several tremendous challenges: Claggett burnt to the ground in 1926; then after it was rebuilt, the school lost its funds twice, once in the Great Depression and once again in a case of embezzlement. Still, against the odds, the school survived, even flourished. Then, in 1955, Father John Owens came to what had become, again, an impoverished and a forgotten place; and again he restored it; he refurbished and built most of our present buildings, and he established our present reputation as one of the finest schools in this area. And each of these men built from within: together with their faculty and with their students, they were themselves the soul of the thing, and gradually the body was regenerated around them.

Certainly, we have been cursed with hard times; but we have also been blessed with great headmasters: men who came young and stayed long; men of vision, determination, and faith—faith in this school certainly, but most of all faith in God, faith in the God to whose glory this school was founded. And this faith remains for this School our only true purpose and our only true hope.

And so, I who share in their faith, stand before you humbled by their example. And thus, I suppose, I do not preach to you at all; I preach only to myself, for I ask myself: how can I be worthy to follow after such faithful and loyal pastors? how can I build on what they have built? how can I preserve what they in faith established?

And, as I look for my answer to these questions, I can think of no better place to look than the place where Kerfoot looked before me, and I can think of no better teacher than his own. Allow me then to end where I began, and

---

[5] David Hein, *A Student's View of The College of St. James on the Eve of the Civil War* (Lewiston, 1988), pp. 21–22.

to quote from Dr. Muhlenberg's final charge to his disciple as he was leaving to found this school:

> *In your station as Principal you will acquire a new experience; you will deal with parents and instructors as well as with pupils. How much wisdom you will need, while you maintain your independence with parents, yet to sympathize with their affection for their children, and make allowance for their blind partialities; and while you support the authority of instructors, to act the paternal part to the boy!*
>
> *But I will not detain you with parting counsels. I had prepared them, but to go over them at this time seemed a piece of formality that would be out of place on this occasion, and quite unnatural considering our past relation. Indeed, all that I could say you have already learned. The rest, only practice can teach you. Experience and your own faithful heart will say to you day by day: Be patient; be kind; be gentle.*[6]

And so, I ask you, please pray for me that I will take these words to heart, so that we together may be the soul of the thing, and the body may again regenerate around us.

Amen.

---

[6] Harrison, i, pp. 53–54.

A Sermon
Preached at the Parish
of Saint John's, Olney

WHEN JOHN ZURN ASKED ME TO PREACH here this morning, he told me that he wanted me to address the question: why Episcopal schools? or more specifically, why does the Episcopal Church need to support its schools? This, I was happy to do, and I am very happy to be with you this morning; but I must warn you, you have asked a teacher a question, and a very interesting question at that, so you may find that you get more of an answer than you bargained for.

Before I begin, let me confess to you that I am in a sense doubly qualified to answer the question which John posed, as I am not only the headmaster of a church school and a former teacher at a different church school, but also the product of two church schools myself. I grew up just outside of Washington; and like my brothers and like my sister, I was (and I suppose always will be) what is sometimes called a "Cathedral brat." I entered Beauvoir in nursery school, and graduated from Saint Albans in the twelfth grade; I spent my entire youth studying in the shadow of the National Cathedral. Indeed, it is worse than that: I was a Cathedral choirboy. And so, I still remember the prayer with which Dr. Callaway began each morning's rehearsal: "May the words of our mouths and the meditations of our hearts be always acceptable in thy sight, oh Lord, our strength and our redeemer. Amen. Now sit down and shut up."

When I went to Saint Albans, Canon Martin still presided as one of the great priest headmasters. I suspect many of you may know of him; he is one of those remarkable Christians who combines great authority with great humility; he reeks integrity. I remember we used to joke that he called God directly on the telephone. And he was always Canon Martin, always a priest, always in his collar. Once I saw him gardening without his collar on, and I was shocked; he was even wearing shorts. And as much as we used to mimic him and laugh about him, we admired him. I would even say we loved him: he was so steady in his purpose, so predictable in his morality, so gracious in his charity. And he preached a very simple gospel, well chosen and directed to the young: choose the hard right against the easy wrong.

And now that I am, myself, a headmaster, indeed, by some strange twist of fate, the headmaster of one of my old school's rivals, I often find myself returning to this gospel and commending it to my own students: don't pick the short cut; don't lie, steal, or cheat; tell the truth, take on the challenge, assume the burden; carry your cross; choose the hard right against the easy wrong.

But it is not just the morality I remember; it is also the community. For the community of my childhood, the community which Canon Martin gathered around him was a wonderful community of brilliant eccentrics, full of laughter, whimsy, and joy; but more than this, it was a loving community which assumed the respect, good will, and affection of its members. And this again is the kind of school I find myself preserving at Saint James. Perhaps even more so, for ours is a smaller school and a boarding school where all of us still fit into the chapel for morning prayer and still fit into the refectory for a single seating and dine family style at smaller tables. And indeed, I like to think that ours is a special kind of school, different from the larger day schools which surround us, a school where no student is lost, a school where every student is given the chance to shine.

And here, I should also mention something which has never struck me as particularly remarkable, but which may strike others who have not attended Episcopal schools as remarkable: Saint James, like Saint Albans, is a community at prayer. Every weekday begins with Chapel at eight. And this is not just some religious assembly; it is worship. We sing a hymn, we hear a lesson from scripture which is considered in a brief address, and we close with three prayers: the prayer for the day, the Lord's Prayer, and the Grace. On Thursdays, we take an hour to celebrate a community Eucharist. And there is, daily, that moment in our common life when I or the chaplain exhort the school as a body: "And we say together, as Our Savior Christ has taught us." And the chapel fills with the regular cadence of the assembled company, most sharing in our common oath of allegiance, all at least considering it: "Thy kingdom come, oh Lord, on earth as it is in heaven."

And I have known this pattern just about all of my life, this regular discipline of common prayer. I knew it at Saint Albans, I knew it when I taught at the Harvard School in Los Angeles, I knew it at General Seminary, and I knew it at Oxford. The only time I did not know it was when I was an undergraduate at Harvard. There we were compartmentalized; religion was a private choice, and a secluded, almost hidden activity. A small group of us would gather in the Episcopal chaplaincy for a Sunday evening Eucharist, but it was not the same. We had retreated into our own Episcopal corner, and everyone else had retreated into their respective corners, the space was empty between us.

And I am used, I suppose, to having this space filled, filled with music, prayer, common sorrow, common laughter, filled because it is made safe, made safe by a strong Episcopal identity, established and protected by our common expectation, our regular, faithful pattern. And so, I am used to common worship, and I know the kind of community which this worship can sustain, a deeper community, a community of individuals certainly, each always worshipping in his or her own way, but a community before God, a community of pilgrims and potential saints, God's own children.

And if there is one thing which I find really dubious in the whole secular approach to life which surrounds us, it is this bizarre notion that religion needs to be purely "private." I myself would reject this doctrine. First of all, it is untrue. If your religion causes you to ignore me, be unkind to me, or God forbid, kill me, then it is as much my business as it is yours. The community has a legitimate interest in the religious beliefs of its individual members.

Secondly, to treat religion only as purely a private choice is to diminish it; it is to reduce it to the level of a commodity. Each of us is left to pick our faith much as we might pick a dandruff shampoo: "here, try this, it will help you look and feel better." Such an approach is particularly disastrous for Christianity, because in Christianity, it is we who are the commodity, not the Faith. We do not choose to follow in the way of the Cross because it is attractive or congenial; we are chosen to follow in the way of the Cross because it is the true way of life revealed to us in the saving story of Jesus Christ. You and I as individual Christians are called by the Faith to "walk in love as Christ loved us," and thus called like him to offer ourselves "as sacrifices unto God." If we insist upon approaching the Faith as a commodity, we will never be real Christians; we will only be users, not followers of the Gospel.

Thirdly, to insist that religion is a purely private matter is to reject the potential for community which a common dedication to the Gospel still offers us, and indeed, all other people of good will who would join us in this common purpose and in this common life. This is why it is good to have a church school; the school itself can become a community which is at once broader in its appeal than a particular parish, but equally committed to the Christian vision of God as love.

Obviously, my school is not entirely Episcopalian, neither is it entirely Christian. I would not wish that it should be; to restrict it in this way would be itself unChristian. But it was founded exactly 150 years ago to be a Church school, and it remains today exactly what it was founded to be: a community inspired by the Christian vision that God is Love. And certainly this vision is an inclusive and a tolerant vision, but it is also a vision which needs to be asserted and defended as the right vision in an increasingly selfish and violent society.

I don't know if you ever saw Harrison Ford in the movie *Witness*, but I think it illustrates my point. Harrison Ford is a Philadelphia police detective long since hardened by the violence of the modern city who goes into hiding with an Amish family to protect their son who was a witness to a murder. The experience of living in a community of faith which rejects violence has a profound affect upon the detective; he is changed. And when the killers come to the community of the Amish to kill him and the boy, ultimately the final killer cannot do it. The witness of the Amish overwhelms him, the burden of his evil is just too heavy to bear when witnessed by a truly good community.

And so, by our own commitment to being communities set apart from the world we too might be capable of a little (very unEpiscopalian) evangelism. For indeed, not everyone comes to us because we are Christian, rather for a less noble motive: they perceive us to be the best means to a more secular end, the best way of preparing their child for college. Still, even though parents send their children for secondary reasons like good order, a general atmosphere of compassion, closer attention to their children, or a better curriculum, their children often leave our schools fundamentally altered by the community of which they have been a part; they leave inspired by the primary reason behind the secondary reasons: they leave inspired by our faith. Certainly, this is what happened to me.

I always remember a junior parents' night at the Harvard School in Los Angeles when I was speaking as the college counselor. I stood up before the gathering of junior parents and assured them that I knew that they wanted their son to go to Harvard as I did (they smiled); to go on to Harvard Graduate School as I did (they smiled even more); maybe even to go on to Oxford as I did (they sat back in their seats and glowed contentment). And then I assured them that I knew that they wanted their son to return as a school teacher and a priest like me. They suddenly looked very uncomfortable, because, of course, that was the last thing they wanted their son to be. So, beware: such can be the effect of a good Episcopal education.

Finally, there is a religious reason why ours is the best sort of education now available to young people in this country; there is a reason why so many non-Episcopalians want to come to our schools, which is itself the direct result of our own Anglican tradition. We are believing humanists, and this means that we recognize the role of both faith and reason in the whole of our human experience: in short, we refuse to take thinking out of believing, or believing out of thinking; each requires each. And it is this, our historic Anglican commitment to the interdependence of faith and reason, which sets us apart from secular humanism on one hand and biblical fundamentalism on the other.

Unlike the secular humanists, we can study the whole of history; we don't have to start at the Enlightenment and avoid dangerous topics like "Judaism," "Islam," and "Christianity," "Catholicism" and "Protestantism," "faith" and "God." We can study important human leaders like Moses and Aaron, Amos and Isaiah, Jesus, Mary, and Paul. We can seek to understand the venture of human faith which has produced the piety of Clare and Francis, the poetry of Milton and Herbert, the heroism of Florence Nightingale and Mother Teresa, the radicalism of Mahatma Gandhi, Martin Luther King, and Desmond Tutu. We can study these people and be challenged by their witness, not just on Sunday but during the week, not just in chapel but in class, not just in religion but in history and in English.

But again, unlike the fundamentalists, we can study the Bible as the very human text which it is; we can consider the differences within it, the changing context of the history which informed it, the distinct voices of its many different authors. And we know the difference between the Bible and a biology text; we know the difference between a poetic description of God's creation and a modern scientific theory of evolution. And we are not afraid: we are not afraid either to consider the theory or to appreciate the poetry. We can do both.

And this I suppose would be my answer to the question of why it is especially incumbent upon us now to preserve our Episcopal schools as our gift to the nation: we need to preserve the middle ground, not just for our children, but for everyone's children, the middle ground where faith and reason can be honored together and thus the whole of our human experience honestly taught and studied. And we need to preserve the holy ground: the ground established by our pious purpose, a common ground where young people can live and work and pray together in a deeper community born of our common discipleship to the Lord of Love.

And this, I think, is what Canon Martin always meant when he spoke of the "hard right against the easy wrong," the message he used to hear from God all those years ago on the telephone: "love the Lord thy God with all thy heart and with all thy soul, and with all thy strength; and love thy neighbor as thyself." For surely, as we seek to teach our young people all that is true and good and beautiful, we can only teach them this.

Amen.

A Sermon
Alumni Weekend Eucharist

"You are the light of the world.
A city built on a hill cannot be hid."
Matthew 5:14

A s we all know, Saint James is a very old school. Now, "very old" is a relative term; we are only "very old" in the American sense. I have, of course, just come from a college in Oxford which was founded in 1423 where I had the care of a chapel which was built in 1630. And so, I suppose, this puts our "oldness"[1] in some perspective.

Still, we are, in the American sense, old. And all of us enjoy the inheritance of this "oldness;" and we bear the duty of piety which this "oldness" brings to us. For you see, we cannot claim this school without constraint: we are not its founders. What we now enjoy, we have in fact largely been given by those who have gone before us. I myself stand before you as the school's tenth headmaster; and this is an especially sobering thought, as I stand in the presence of the school's eighth headmaster, a priest whose devotion to this school and to its vision stands as an inspiration to us all.

And being as I am very conscious of his great record of stewardship and service before me, I asked Father Owens if he would preach instead of me; but he (rather typically) refused. "No, Stuart," he said, "I think they would rather hear from you."

And isn't this a remarkable thought? They would rather hear from me after only one year as headmaster and not Father Owens after some twenty-nine? Surely, we should draw our wisdom from a deeper well?

---

[1] My English Chair, Mr. Collin, claims that "oldness" is not a word. I refer him to Shakespeare's use in *Lear*, Act 1, Scene 2, line 50: "Keeps our fortunes from us till our oldness cannot relish them."

But still, he has a point. The question before us now is not so much what has Saint James been, but rather what has Saint James become. What is it now? what will it be in its future? And so, as the School's present headmaster, it falls to me to preach this morning.

And here, I am reminded of a letter from an alumnus which greeted me upon my arrival as headmaster. He wrote that he enjoyed alumni weekend very much, except for one thing; he did not have a chance to meet many students. And I remember thinking at the time: here is the good alumnus; not the bad alumnus who returns just to relive old memories and retrieve past times, but the good alumnus who comes to do these things, but also to see the present and help build for the future.

And certainly, we would do well on this occasion to remind ourselves that good schools are not museums. They are not static and frozen in time; they are living, developing communities which grow and change. And the time of a student amongst us is as it has always been: short. The School hymn puts it only too well: "time like and ever-rolling stream bears all its sons away."

And of course our reading from Ecclesiasticus reminds us that all of life is like that: each of us lives within our generation and can only leave a testament behind us. Some "have left behind a name, so that others declare their praise. But of others there is no memory; they have perished as though they had never been."

Every alumnus (and now also alumna) knows the feeling of that first visit back to School: "it's not mine anymore; there are new buildings; old buildings are used differently; my friends have left; many of my teachers have left also; and those who remain are my teachers no more."

But yet, to insist that Saint James needs to change and to develop as a living community is not to suggest that we are free to stray from the vision which first inspired our founding and then continued to inspire our past; we are not.

For this is holy ground: made holy by the vision which built these buildings upon this hill and called generations of students to live and to study here. It is ground set aside for a holy purpose: to teach and to inspire the young.

And note that I say both teach and inspire. Some schools seek to teach well, but few schools seek to teach and to inspire well; we are one of these. We do not exist merely to teach English, math, science, language, history, and art, though we are proud to teach these things. We exist to inspire a particular use for this knowledge: the pursuit of goodness, the worship of Christ in our fellows, the loving imitation of the saints of God.

And this is why we bear the name of a saint, Saint James of Jerusalem, the brother of our Lord, one who lived for his faith, and even died for it. All of us who are gathered here are meant to leave this place resolved to be like Saint James, resolved to be faithful: visionaries, prophets, dreamers of dreams, even martyrs. This is the vision of this school, this is the hope which has been kindled here in a thousand faithful hearts.

But how do we put this in a brochure? How do we sell this vision in a society which appears to have strayed from a faith which requires self-discipline and self-offering? I do not always know. It is indeed a tremendous challenge.

But I do know this. As soon as we stray from this vision, the moment we give in to the temptation to be a school like any other school, we have lost. We have lost what we have been given by those who have gone before us; and even worse, lost what we can give to those who will come after us.

And lest you doubt my resolve in this, allow me to tell you a story.

In my first week as headmaster, I was faced with a minor hazing incident to which I responded with some severity; obviously, not a quiet beginning for a new headmaster. Still, I perceived a point of principle which threatened the founding vision of the school. How could we call ourselves a Church school? how could we bear the name of a Christian saint? worship in this chapel and gather at this altar if we allowed such willful acts of cruelty amongst us? however misguided or innocent the intent?

But my stance in this, as in some other things, was perceived to be a change. But this in itself was distressing, because mine was not a change away from our vision, but a change back to our vision, a change back to the purpose of our founding, the purpose of our being, the whole reason for our existence.

Still, it was a change. And it was greeted with some resistance. I remember meeting with my prefects afterwards and listening to their bewilderment: "You can't do this, Father. You are taking away our privileges. Everyone will leave the school." "Fine," I said, "let them leave." "But then the school will close." "Fine," I said, "let it close. This school exists for a purpose. It exists for the glory of God. If it can only exist as a haven for cowards and bullies, then I say close it."

A new headmaster, yes; but in another sense, the same headmaster. For this new headmaster faces the same threat every headmaster has faced before me: everyone will leave; no one will come. And this is a threat which can come from any source: the rebellious student, the angry parent, even the self-righteous alumnus, each pursuing his or her own private agenda, each seeking in some small way to warp the vision to serve his or her own particular need, his or her own particular desire. But the answer to this threat must always be the same: so what? This school is not a student-led school; it is not a parent-led school; it is not an alumni-led school. It is a vision-led school. And this is what makes it great. Certainly, this is why I left Oxford to come to it, and this is why all of us have come to it, even sometimes without realizing why we have come. Saint James is different; and as long as we remain different, as long as we remain faithful, there will be others like us who will come also.

But the moment we lose faith, the moment we forget why we are here, and seek to serve the school as an end in itself, we have sunken into idolatry. We have begun to worship a school instead of the God the school was founded to serve.

When I first went to see Father Owens just after I had assumed my duties as headmaster, he offered me some encouragement: "You are young, Stuart." "Father, is there not something more encouraging you could say?" He paused and considered the case, then answered, "You are young, Stuart." He might have added foolish, which is of course part of the same virtue.

Later, in a subsequent conversation, he offered some advice drawn from his own experience facing the very same challenges I face now: "I never really worried if I was popular, I just tried to do what I thought was right." So must I, even as he did.

My own old headmaster, Canon Martin, used to say to us in chapel: "Choose the hard right against the easy wrong." And now, I hear his voice, as I say the same to my students in Chapel. And I hear the voice of my students as they pray every morning: "thy will be done on earth as it is heaven." And I pray for them, even as I pray with them: help them to mean it, oh Lord, help them really to mean it; for we have need of what we pray for.

Let this school be, oh God, just what it was meant to be: a "city built on a hill" which "cannot be hid." And fill us with your light, that all may see it here and rejoice at its brightness. And so inspire us with your love that we who would bear the name of a saint may each of us grow like him into the likeness of the one he served, even Jesus "the pioneer and perfecter of our faith." For to this faith you have called us, in this faith you have taught us, and by this faith we have been forever changed.

Amen.

A LETTER TO PARENTS
CONCERNING THE SCHOOL BONFIRE

Dear Parents:

This past Friday, 15 October, the students held a bonfire. Earlier in the week, I had expressed concerns about this bonfire, specifically, its safety, the language used in cheers, and adherence to the school's rules. When I suggested to the prefects that the bonfire should be better supervised with the faculty invited to attend, they insisted that this would be a break with "tradition" and that it would ruin the "spirit" of the event. In fact, some parents even called to support the prefects' position.

After several conversations with the senior prefect and the prefect council during the week, I agreed that they could be responsible for the bonfire as they requested, and they agreed that the bonfire would be well conducted. Specifically, they promised me that there would be no alcohol. The bonfire was to last one hour and to take place on the lower soccer field; the prefects were aware that two faculty were assigned to the back porch of Claggett, available should any difficulties arise. I was working in my office.

While I was working, I was distressed to hear the cheers; they were obscene. Still, I decided that this would be a matter we would have to address next year. After an hour, the senior prefect came to report to me that the bonfire had "gone well."

During the weekend, several teachers and parents expressed the concern that they had heard stories of widespread cigarette smoking and some drinking as well. When I looked into the matter, I discovered that the stories were justified.

Obviously, I had made the wrong decision. I had believed the prefects, and I had entrusted them with too much responsibility. The event was not properly supervised, and this is my fault. Still, the rules of the school are clear, and many students used their freedom to break them; this cannot be excused. I was particularly horrified to learn that three prefects were themselves drinking. Let me assure you that they are no longer prefects; the senior prefect has also resigned; they have all apologized to the school.

Recognizing my own responsibility in this and anxious to find out exactly what had happened so that I could inform you, I offered to forego the usual punishment of suspension or expulsion for drinking if the students involved turned themselves in. By this means, I have been able to compile a list which I think is reasonably complete. They will be placed on probation, and the chaplain is exploring a suitable community service project.

Again, I thank you for your support. I apologize again for my decision and for its consequences. As headmaster, I seek to find the same middle ground in the shepherding of my students that you as parents would seek to find at home. On one hand, I want to trust my students and give them more responsibility; on the other, I must always remember that they are adolescents and therefore need to be protected from the appeal of the crowd. It is sad to think, of course, that when we err on the side of trust, we suffer the greatest consequences. Still, we learn from our mistakes, and we move on. Together, we shall get it right.

Yours faithfully,

The Revd. Dr. D. Stuart Dunnan
The Headmaster, Saint James School

A Sermon
At the Founder's Eucharist

Surely, the Lord is in this place; and I did not know it.
Genesis 28:16

SCHOOL IS A BUSY PLACE. There is always something to do. For faculty, there are the countless tasks of a "triple threat" boarding school: teaching, coaching, dorm life. There are classes, papers, comments, study halls, practices, games, trips, dorm duties: in short, a hundred tasks. And then there is that one conversation with a student which really means something, that class when they suddenly get it, that game when they really play beyond themselves, that play when they really perform.

There are those moments in a teacher's busy life when the tasks of teaching fade away and the purpose of teaching becomes clear. We always know it; we never really forget it; but somehow we lose sight of it: teaching is a vocation; what we do is wonderful.

And so also for students, school is a busy place. There is too much homework; the tests are too hard; the practices too long; the games too tough. There is always too much to do. For indeed, part of growing up, part of a good education at a good school requires that students be challenged in just this kind of way. School is when students learn that they cannot do everything that they want to do; sometimes they have to choose. Do I write for the newpaper or sing in the choir? Do I do one assignment perfectly or both assignments less than perfectly? Do I go to the movies or stay behind to work on a history paper? These are the choices which students have to make.

And through it all, as students make the gradual progression up the ranks from the front pews towards the back pews and then out the doors of this chapel on that day in June, they learn about the world and about themselves. But they are usually too busy, too involved in the process of their learning, to realize what their learning is for. Thus, it is most probably when they have gone, when they have graduated, that they will begin to realize what happened to them here: the teachers who affected them and changed their lives for good, the friendships which they made here, the real friendships, the deep, strong, wonderful friendships of their youth.

And then they will come back as alumni, and they will walk around this school, visit their old room where they once studied and slept, walk along the fields where they once played, sit at a desk. And maybe they will wander into this chapel, not because they have to, but because once they had to, every morning, here is where they gathered, here as a school with their teachers and their friends. And maybe they will light a candle, just to remember their time together here and to note a truth: "Surely, the Lord is in this place; and I did not know it."

You see, all of us are a bit like Jacob on his journey to Haran, all of us—teachers, students, parents; all of us have come together at this moment and in this place, because we are, each of us, also on a journey, a journey like his: a journey into our futures, a journey into the unknown.

And so, like him, we proceed in faith, each of us, task to task, challenge to challenge. But as we attend to these tasks and meet these challenges, we run a great risk, the risk that we will forget that we are on a journey in the first place and that this school which we now share will be ours together for only a very short time.

On this day especially, we remember the others who have gone before us, not just students, but also parents, friends, and faculty, all of whom remembered this school as important in their lives and therefore gave of their substance to sustain and to preserve it for us and for our benefit. We give thanks to God for their foresight and their vision, a vision like Jacob's, a vision setting this place apart as significant on their journey, the place where they learned something about themselves, something about their futures, where they learned that they were journeying for a purpose, and not journeying alone.

For like us, they shared this place. Together, they learned here; they grew in the challenges of youth; they made friends; they tested and discovered themselves; they strove for what is good. And then, they journeyed on, carrying their vision out into the world, forward into the future.

To quote the hymn we just sang:

These stones that have echoed their praises are holy,
And dear is the ground where their feet have once trod;
Yet here they confessed they were strangers and pilgrims,
And still they were seeking the city of God.

(William Draper, 1855–1933)

And even as we are not the first; so also, we are not the last; others will follow after us; and like us and those before us, they will learn here too. And even though the tasks may change and the challenges take on new dimensions, the place itself will remain a place set apart. A place set apart for students and teachers to learn and grow together, to experience again every year the magic of youth: its growth, its progress, its promise.

And let us hope that there will always be visionaries amongst us like Jacob who will take the time to rest on their journey, to dream and see the angels of God. For this is indeed a place where God has rested his ladder; it is a magical place, full of all the magical opportunities to learn and to grow which only angels bring and carry with them back and forth to heaven.

What am I asking for? Only this: value this school and value your time here; honour your friendships, relish your tasks, discover your gifts. Stop, look, see where you are. Know it for the holy place that it is. And busy as you are, forget not what your busyness is meant to be about. Remember to dream, and in your dreams to look, for it is all too easy to forget to dream, and thus to fail to look, and not looking, to trip; for you see, there is a ladder right here, standing just in front of us, and reaching up to heaven. But we need to dream to see it.

Amen.

AN ESSAY
WRITTEN FOR THE MID-ATLANTIC
EPISCOPAL SCHOOL ASSOCIATION

WHAT MAKES US EPISCOPALIAN?

AT A MEETING OF THE MAESA BOARD, I was asked to write down a few thoughts in response to the question: what makes our schools "Episcopalian"? The answer of course is not as obvious as it may sound. Each of our member schools is in fact quite different: some are day schools, some boarding; some elementary, some middle, some high schools; some are single sex, some coeducational. Each of us has our own character, our own history, our own mission. And yet there is this word which unites us: "Episcopal." We share a common "Episcopalian" inheritance, a common "Episcopalian" identity.

So what does this inheritance mean? What does this identity bring to us? I would offer the following thoughts based upon my own experience here at Saint James, at Harvard School in Los Angeles where I started teaching, and at Saint Albans (and Beauvoir before that) where I was myself a student.

First of all, Episcopal schools are by their very nature *inclusive*. This goes to the very core of our Anglican identity. Unlike other churches in the Reformation, the Church of England was an *inclusive* church: everyone in England was meant to be included. Indeed, Elizabeth I is well remembered for her remark that she did not intend "to pry into men's souls." Therefore, as Anglicans in America, Episcopalians do not have the same strong confessional identity as Roman Catholics on one hand or more evangelical or fundamentalist Protestants on the other, and the culture of our schools reflects this confessional latitude. Whereas other Christian churches have established their schools to protect their children from society at large, we have established our schools as part of our mission to society at large, to better educate all children, not just our own. In fact, we believe that good education requires a diverse community not just culturally, racially, and economically, but religiously as well. Episcopal schools, therefore, admit students and hire faculty who are not Episcopalian; this is a part of our more inclusive Anglican understanding of our witness to Christ, and thus of our mission.

Second, we are schools with *values*. We have certain expectations for our students and our faculty which are based upon our *belief* in what is right and what is wrong. Thus, as Episcopal schools, we *believe* that it is wrong for us to tolerate lying, stealing, or cheating within our communities; it is wrong to tolerate bullying or cruelty of any kind. We *believe* that we have a duty to challenge our students to be better people, as we *believe* "better" to be. We do not want them to be bigoted or selfish or fearful; we want them to "walk in love as Christ loved us and gave himself for us, an offering and a sacrifice to God." Thus, we want them to be courageous; indeed, to be faithful.

Third, we are *believing humanists*. We come from a tradition which pursues a humanist understanding of Faith and a faithful understanding of human beings. We value faith in God as part of the human venture of life, and we value human beings as "made in the image of God." Thus, as believers, we study religion and ethics; these are not just personal matters, they are common matters to be studied. We study the full spectrum of literature, the full record of history. And also, as humanists, we are not afraid to use our minds, to adopt the empirical method and study what the world presents to us. We do not reject reason for faith or faith for reason; we embrace them both, together.

Fourth, we *worship*; and this is perhaps what is most important about us. We gather in one place in a regular pattern as a community to pause and be together, to consider our state as people in the world, our obligations to each other, our hopes, our fears, our very nature as human beings. And we *pray* to God; we pray in our tradition, not claiming to practice any other, but only our own, and asking in humility that all who are with us will join with us as much as they can, each according to his or her own conscience, so that we can pray and sing and laugh and cry together; all of us, fellow pilgrims in the common way of life.

These would be my thoughts; I wonder, would they be yours? Could they be the beginning of a useful definition of what it means to be an "Episcopal" school?

Fall 1993

A Sermon
Preached at Saint John's
Parish, Hagerstown

Jesus said, "What do you think?
A man had two sons . . ."
Matthew 21:28

VER SINCE I BECAME A HEADMASTER (which is to say during this past year), preaching has taken on a whole new meaning. First of all, I don't have enough time. I think back longingly to my days as an Oxford chaplain when I could clear my desk of research and set aside a day or so to prepare. No such luck now. There are meetings to attend, trips to make, phone calls to answer, letters to write, chapels to lead, classes to teach, games to watch, students and teachers to encourage, appreciate, support, direct, consider. I don't think my desk has been cleared since I arrived, and I don't think that it ever will. Being a headmaster is a bit like flying into a black hole; there is always somewhere to go, something to do, and there is always a certain feeling of mild panic: what do I do now? which of the six things I am supposed to be doing should I do?

So, preparing for this sermon meant stealing some time before the football game yesterday morning, going to my office, shoving all my work to a new corner of my desk, next to the work from last week, and hoping that I would only be interrupted once every half hour instead of the usual once every five minutes. Saturday mornings can often be fairly productive; the students are usually asleep.

But then, as I think about it, I suppose that being a headmaster is a bit like being a rector, or a lawyer, or a doctor, or nurse, or a carpenter, or a mother or a father, or even really the usual combination of several of these things which most people attempt to do these days. It is difficult for all of us to take the

24

time to sit and think and pray a while. This is, I think, one of the great spiritual challenges of our age, each of us separated and lost, caught in our own busyness. So, I come to you, I suppose, as something of a "wounded healer," someone caught on the hop by the message of this Sunday's gospel, forced to stop and consider it quickly; perhaps too quickly, but certainly intensely as the pre-sermon adrenaline flowed, and at least a day earlier, even if the moment was a stolen one and the demands of a busy Saturday afternoon pressed in upon me.

And as I considered the text from this morning's Gospel, the second great difference which comes from being a headmaster also came into play.

When I used to hear these parables about the father and his sons or the master and his servants, I always used to focus on the son or on the servant: which son am I? which servant am I? And this of course is proper and the way in which one should think about these parables. The father or the master is meant to be God, and the sons or the servants are meant to be us, each of us considering whether we are good children or good servants of God. I think of the name of one of the oldest and most distinguished societies within the Church, "the Daughters of the King;" I think of the prayer which Jesus most especially taught us how to pray: "Our Father, who art in heaven."

And so, as we hear Our Lord's parable in this morning's Gospel about a man who has two sons, one who says he will do his father's bidding and then doesn't and one who refuses and does, we are meant to focus on the two sons and to ask ourselves: which one are we? the good one or the bad one?

And certainly, this is what I have always done. But now that I am a headmaster, and particularly the headmaster of a boarding school and therefore in place of a parent for some 150 adolescent girls and boys, I suddenly find myself focusing on the father in the story much more than I ever did before. For now that it is my job to inspire and to direct the young, and thereby help to love them into goodness, I must admit that I have a lot more sympathy, even empathy if you will, for God's role in our salvation.

Am I the good son or the bad son? I don't know. I know that I try to be the good son and that I want to be the good son; but this is a challenging parable, and I am sure that it hits all of us right where it hurts: all of us as practicing Christians are often guilty of saying one thing to God in this church on Sunday morning and then going out there and doing something else in the world. The challenge to do the will of God is a challenge to be perfect "even as our heavenly father is perfect;" and I don't know about any of you, but I can just speak for myself when I say that I am not there yet. Certainly, I am trying, but I am not perfect as God is perfect. Now maybe some of you are and perhaps I should allow a moment for you to stand up and tell us how you achieved this, but let's be honest: anyone who would claim to be the perfect disciple, the perfect child of God, is obviously a fraud. The very claim itself reveals a sinful lack of humility and a real failure to accept and understand one's self as a fallible and feeble vessel for God's grace.

And certainly this is our Lord's point: beware the hypocrites; beware the sanctimonious practicers of religion who have yet to appreciate the real challenges of faith. Beware the ones who claim to be saints; for if they were saints, they would never claim to be.

Now, here I reveal my age and speak to my generation and perhaps also those of you who raised us and watched a little television with us. Doesn't the bad son in this parable remind you of Eddie Haskell in *Leave it to Beaver*? "Oh yes, Mrs. Cleaver, whatever you say, Mrs. Cleaver, my father always says . . ." And doesn't the good son remind you of Wally or even Beaver? Don't you remember how Eddie would always say the right thing and do the wrong thing, whereas Wally and especially Beaver would always say the wrong thing but then sometimes do the right thing? Which was the better son? And didn't the show always make us feel good, because that's what we were like ourselves? Disagreeing with our parents, challenging our parents, sometimes getting into trouble, but always in some sense trying to be good?

And now that I am a headmaster, I find myself feeling a bit like the Cleavers, with a fair number of Wallys in the family, a larger number of Beavers, and a few Eddie Haskells as well. Therefore, I now find myself focusing on the father and feeling for God in this parable in a way in which I never really felt for God before. For now that I am a headmaster, I have discovered that I don't just love my Wallys and my Beavers; I love my Eddie Haskells as well. I don't trust them in the same way, I worry for them, I tend to be especially anxious about them, but I don't love them any less than the others. I sometimes think that I love them more, probably because they need me more, rely upon me more, are less than steady without me.

And think back to *Leave it to Beaver*. Eddie was a part of that family. June and Ward certainly had his number and did not particularly trust him; but they were fond of him, cared for him, even looked out for him. And through it all, they preserved a relationship with him which was sincere and deep and strong and loving.

I think of a recent experience with one of my students who was demerited by a teacher for smoking off campus at a school party. Now, four demerits are no minor matter; they are four hours on work squad, so he was not pleased. He came to see me furious that he should be given demerits for smoking when he was not even at school. I explained to him that the school reserved the right to defend its good name and that he was being punished for besmirching it. And then it was my turn to challenge him: I told him that I was disappointed in him because he had told me just the last week that he had given up smoking, and therefore he had lied to me. Later, he came back to apologize, and he came back again to speak of other things.

What was important in this exchange was not so much his bad act, but rather the good relationship between us; this is what both of us knew we needed to mend and to preserve. So, in the end, it was the lie, the deceit, that counted, not so much the bad deed itself. The deed had been done and accounted for, the lie could live forever. For you see, the act only disobeyed love, the lie denied it. And so it is for us with God; it is the relationship which counts, and that relationship requires a real commitment to honesty and to trust.

And this I suppose is the Good News according to a much harried headmaster: God our heavenly Father loves us, even when we fail him, even when we speak and act against him. God still loves us, maybe even all the more intensely. Only remember the words of St. Paul in that wonderful passage from his letter to the Philippians which we just heard: "If there is any encouragement in Christ, any incentive of love, any participation in the Spirit, any affection and sympathy, complete my joy by being of the same mind, having the same love, being in full accord and of one mind. Do nothing from selfishness or conceit, but in humility count others better than yourselves. Let each of you look not only to your own interests, but also to the interests of others." (Philippians 2:1–4)

For indeed, even if each of us is at times something of an Eddie Haskell, we are still a part of the family, still welcomed, and still loved, even loved as ourselves especially.

Amen.

A Sermon
Preached in the Chapel of
Lincoln College, Oxford

For though I am absent in body, yet I am with you in spirit,
rejoicing to see your good order and the firmness of your
faith in Christ.
Colossians 2:5

ET ME BEGIN BY THANKING the chaplain for his gracious invitation to preach to you this evensong. As you know, it is a real pleasure for me to be back where I served so happily as chaplain myself. Let me also take this occasion to thank Father Robin for his kind words in the *College Record*; it was typically gracious of him to write as he did.

It was exactly two years ago this week that I received a phone call asking if I would leave this good place and return to America to serve as headmaster of Saint James School, so it is a special privilege for me to be back here with so many friends whom I have missed so very much. It is a special privilege to be back to hear the College Choir which the rector and I connived to build so successfully and a special privilege to be back with all of you now in your third year whom I remember welcoming in your first. I made a promise to myself that I would try to see you again before you left; I am glad that I have kept it; I look forward to being with you this week.

And so, I return from a distance of space and time to this pulpit and to this chapel which seem to me so very familiar, to faces many so well known and so well-beloved.

Now, I choose my words on purpose: well-beloved.

In the passage from his epistle to the Colossians which we just heard read, St. Paul speaks with real affection of the community he has left behind:

"For though I am absent in body, yet I am with you in spirit." Obviously, I would say the same of this community; and not only the community of this chapel, but also the wider community of this college of which I was once a part.

Certainly, it is one of the great ironies of life that we never fully appreciate how deeply we have committed ourselves to those around us until it is time to part. Sadly, it is at that time that we realize the importance of our friendships, the depth of our need and our affection.

Indeed, it is often only the occasion of our parting which will force us to express how much we have meant to each other in our life together and how much we hope that we will continue to mean to each other in our life apart. Coming here reminds me of many such conversations and the deeper friendships which have followed.

And now, of course, I am part of a different community serving in a different role: no longer chaplain, but headmaster; no longer everybody's friend, if you will, but as it was once described to me, "everybody's boss."

In the life of a small boarding school, the headmaster's power is tremendous. Every teacher is on an annual contract. I determine who is hired and who stays. I determine how much everyone is paid. I determine what they teach and where they live. All students are admitted under my authority and remain under my authority.

And so, in my life, I have gone from a community in which I served as everybody's brother to a community in which I serve as everybody's father; and for an affectionate fellow like me, this has been challenging, particularly last year when I was new and perceived the need to "tighten up" and make some difficult decisions which were not universally popular. And, as you know, I rather like to be popular, so it was a hard year.

But to say it was a hard year is not to say that it was not a good year; it was. I was able to accomplish a great deal. I was able to turn the school around and begin to build a better place. And in this effort, in my effort to do this good, I began to make a different kind of connection with teachers and students and members of the wider school community who rejoiced at the good being accomplished and stepped forward to help me.

And so, now I find myself yet again deeply committed to a community and deeply committed to the individuals within it, just as I was to all of you, but in a different role. And I have found at Saint James the same great truth which I found here at Lincoln: the spirit of community is love.

I love my teachers and I love my students; I don't always give them what they want; and therefore I am not myself always popular; but I love them with real devotion. I run the school for their good as I perceive it; I wish them well.

And I choose the word: love. This is the imperative; this is what Christians are called to do; this is the way towards purpose, the way towards meaning, the way of life which Christ has shown to us.

And I don't mean love in the sentimental sense: merely I like you, and you like me. I mean love in the moral sense: I am committed to you; and thus committed to what is good for you. It matters not if you like me, it matters only if I have served you faithfully.

Now I make this point and I preach this sermon, because it seems to me that just about all of you will assume similar positions in your lives. In your family life, most of you will be mothers and fathers; in your professional life, teachers, medical doctors, solicitors and barristers, managers, owners, and executives. In all of these roles, you will need to assume real authority and exercise real power for the sake of the whole community you serve and for the good of the individuals within it, and this will mean that you may not always do what is popular.

Be prepared to make this sacrifice, and worry not; worry only that you do what is right, that you have loved those given to your care with all the ability and all the commitment which you can muster. And remember: the Christian imperative to love is a moral and not a sentimental one. Play to God; play not to the crowd.

And if you have done what is right, or at least attempted what is right, you will be respected for this, even admired, and the commitment between you and the people you serve will become, in the end, all the stronger. For in the end, it is this commitment which counts; and it is only this commitment which is the proof of love.

Amen.

Summer 1994

A Letter
Concerning the Testament
of John Ferguson

Dear Friends:

On 7 June 1994, an alumnus of the School, John Ferguson, class of 1932, died after a long struggle with cancer. He will be greatly missed by his neighbors and his friends, his Saint James classmates prominent amongst them. He was a delightful man with a keen mind, a playful wit, and a faithful, loyal nature. He was particularly faithful in his care for his wife, Betty, who was often unwell during their marriage and who predeceased him in 1971. It was an honor for me to officiate at Mr. Ferguson's memorial service in Pittsburgh and to bury his ashes next to his wife here in Hagerstown.

Mr. Ferguson was also very faithful to Saint James School. This is why I write to you. By provision of his will, the School will receive property in the amount of some two million dollars to be "a permanent endowment fund . . . to be used for the enhancement of the salaries of the teaching staff of Saint James School." This bequest is typical of Mr. Ferguson: perceptive, generous, and unassuming. Indeed, it is remarkable to note that a man capable of conceiving and giving such a substantial gift continued to live modestly in a two-bedroom house in a quiet Pittsburgh suburb.

As Admiral Holloway wrote to you in the most recent edition of the *Saint James Review*, the Board of Trustees has adopted a master plan which addresses our continuing need for capital improvements in the next few years. We are just now completing the renovation of the Cotton Building to house the Bowman-Byron Fine Arts Center. With the help of our friends, we hope to proceed to other projects: the renovation of Kemp Hall as a student center, a new library, and the renovation of the main dormitory. Obviously, the need to increase our endowment is equally pressing, and this remarkable gift from a thoughtful alumnus could not be more welcome.

In order to remember Mr. Ferguson and to honor his memory at the School, the Board has approved the establishment of two endowed chairs to be given to "those two members of the faculty who in the opinion of the headmaster contribute the most to the education of our students and the quality of our life as a school. In this way, the name of John Ferguson shall be remembered amongst us in association with our finest and our best."

It is good to know that a man who gave so generously to us will always be remembered here with admiration and with gratitude, and that a man who died without children has gained in the end a whole host of children: indeed, generations upon generations. May his soul rest in peace, and may light perpetual shine upon him.

Yours faithfully,

The Revd. Dr. D. Stuart Dunnan
The Headmaster, Saint James School

Spring 1995

A Sermon
at the Eucharist of Thanksgiving
for our Founders and Benefactors

Every generous act of giving with every perfect
gift comes from above . . .
James 1:17

DO NOT KNOW IF MANY OF YOU have had occasion to consider the School's motto recently, but I thought it appropriate on this occasion to pause and to reflect upon its meaning.

Ours is a very interesting motto, chosen from the passage in the Epistle of Saint James which we have just heard read. This, of course, is appropriate because Saint James is our patron: his words in the original Greek are inscribed around the school's seal.

Now, the fact that our motto is in Greek and is written within the larger context of the apostle's letter makes its meaning a little less immediate. First of all, we have to translate it into English, and then we have to consider just what it is that the apostle is trying to say.

The translation is important, because I think that the English is sometimes misleading. The Greek is more usually translated "every good gift," and this is a good translation, except that it gives the impression that Saint James is speaking of a gift, a thing given, when really he is speaking of the act of giving, the motion, the purpose, the intent to give as well; hence the better translation "every generous act of giving." And this better translation points to what the apostle is trying to tell us.

Anyone hearing this passage just superficially would think that Saint James is being pious. He is simply saying after the manner of many pious and religious people, that all good gifts come from God, not from us; we are only

33

His instruments. We have all heard pious people speak in this way, denying themselves as a way of asserting how much they love God. Thus, we can reject our motto as an expression of the apostle's piety, the apostle, if you will, just trying to show off, just trying to show that he loves God more than himself.

Thought of in this way, our motto is not a very compelling one, it does not really travel well outside the chapel, and it does not really challenge us to lead a different kind of life. Indeed, even within the chapel, it rings a little hollow: surely, if I give a good gift, it comes from me, as well as from God; I do not need to deny my own responsibility for my own actions just to give God the credit. Surely God is bigger than that: I can love Him and myself; the good gift can be mine and His as well.

But to think of our motto in this way is to completely lose Saint James's point. He is not speaking of gifts as passive things which come only from God and not from us. He is describing for us the very life of God, the purpose of God, that one great verb of love which is revealed to us in the actions of God the Father, God the Son, and God the Holy Spirit, God in His three persons who has made us, redeemed us, and sanctifies us.

And so, by insisting that the nature of God is this action of love and this purpose of giving, Saint James is able to invite us into the life of God with the simplest of invitations: be generous; give. Thus, the apostle is inviting us to give of our treasure and our time and our talent not merely because of the good we will accomplish, but rather more because of the good purpose of God which we will experience in our giving.

The truth which Saint James is seeking to teach those of us who will bear his name in the world is simply this: if you want to find meaning in life, joy and fulfillment, if you want to really live life as it is meant to be lived at its fullest, then be generous; live your life generously. As Saint Paul put it, "walk in love as Christ loved us and gave himself up for us, an offering and a sacrifice to God." Or as Our Lord put it, "it is more blessed to give than to receive."

When I stand as a priest at this altar and assume the role of Christ and repeat his words, when I take the bread and break it and call the bread his body, when I take the wine and call the wine his blood, and then when I take what he has called his body and his blood and I share these gifts with all of you his people, I am humbled every time. I am humbled, because I stand at the door of heaven, I stand right here offering the invitation to everlasting life, real life,

life as Christ himself lived it, the life of God as each of us can know it, life broken and taken and given away.

And when I look at our teachers and consider the kind of sacrifice that all of them make to live on this hill and to give their lives so fully to their students, I am humbled again. When I think of the money and the worldly glory which they have chosen to forego, when I think of their dedication and their sacrifice, I find myself on holy ground.

I think of the young master in the early hours of the morning dealing with a problem on his hall after a full day and a full evening of teaching and coaching, knowing that after only a few hours of sleep he will be up in time for chapel and his first period class only to be told by half his class that they did not have time to do his homework.

When I think of what it means to teach here, I see again that door, that invitation, that life of giving which speaks to us of the very life of God.

When I think of Mr. Hoyer and how he has remained here faithfully teaching for 36 years, watching others come and go, but staying here himself, I see a testament to our faith, a living example of what our motto is meant to be about: live your life generously. And if you know Mr. Hoyer, then you know that he has not always found his work in this place to be easy, but he has always found it worthwhile, worth doing, delighting in his students, regretting their failures, rejoicing in their accomplishments; and thus, finding here real joy.

This whole school stands as a real and tangible testament to the truth which Saint James would teach us. Our buildings, our playing fields, our very foundation, all of this was given by those who found real joy in giving, those who found in the mission of this place a real opportunity to give generously and thus to live more deeply in the life of God.

And the students who come here come because they are sent here by parents and by patrons who want them to be educated and nurtured and directed aright, and who give gladly of their substance and of their treasure, sometimes at great sacrifice for their children's sake.

And again, I am humbled, and the more thoughtful of our students are humbled also: they know that they are loved. I had a boy just the other day in my office who spoke to me very movingly of the great gratitude he felt towards his father who has paid his tuition and given him the opportunity to come to Saint James. He spoke of his father's generosity as a great trust, and thus of his own responsibility to be worthy of his father's sacrifice. Again, there I was on holy ground.

People ask me why I do not hesitate in my duty as headmaster to ask for support in my hopes for Saint James. The answer is really a basic one: I am a Christian; and as a Christian, I believe that it is good to give. In fact, I believe that it is essential.

And I know that there are some who will avoid me for this reason; they are well advised to do so. They will go along to the new arts center and see that list of names and see their friends and classmates and think, "whew, I got away." And during the years ahead, they will go to other buildings and see other lists with other names and feel relieved that theirs is absent. And I am sorry for them, sorry that they have failed to give generously of course, but really sorry that they are failing to live their lives with the kind of joyful purpose which Christ himself has shown to us to be the only way for us to live our lives, if we are to live them well.

A student asked me recently what I wanted my students to be after they graduated, "only two things," I said, "honest and generous." "Ah, Father," she said, "you would say that." "Yes," I said, "and I will always say that, as did Saint James." "Saint James? what do you mean?" "Look it up," I said, "but you need to know your Greek."

Amen.

Fall 1995

An Essay
To Answer the Challenge:
"I would never send my child to
boarding school."

Written for the Vincent/Curtis Educational Register

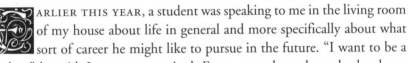ARLIER THIS YEAR, a student was speaking to me in the living room of my house about life in general and more specifically about what sort of career he might like to pursue in the future. "I want to be a teacher," he said. I was not surprised. Even as an eleventh grader he shows many of the characteristics of a good teacher: he is considerate of his class-mates, committed to the school as a community, and genuinely anxious to do what is right and what is good. He is, in short, what my headmaster used to call "a fine young man." And as my headmaster knew then and I know now, all fine young people consider teaching if they feel supported and appreciated within the community of their school.

I then asked him in what sort of school he would like to teach: a day school or a boarding school? His answer was quick and definite: "a boarding school." "Why?" I asked. And here his answer captured the heart of what I would like to say in this essay: "I want to know my students, like you know me."

If I were to point to what is different between a boarding school and a day school, I would say that it is just this: the greater bond which exists between us as we live together on the same campus, and thus the stronger feeling of community which our stronger relationships provide.

The bonds of friendship which exist between students at boarding school are inevitably stronger, just as the bonds are stronger between teachers; we are not just colleagues, but friends and neighbors. But more importantly, the

37

teaching relationship, the bond between student and teacher is stronger. Boarding faculty do not just teach in the classroom; we teach on the playing fields, in our houses and in our apartments, in the dormitories, at the dinner table, in the school van on a trip. We are with our students when they are serious and determined, thoughtful and philosophical, foolish and stupid, charming and funny. We know them and we care for them *in loco parentis*, in place of their parents, not replacing their parents, but acting for their parents: advising them, supporting them, disciplining them; sometimes saying no to them, and sometimes saying yes.

Anyone who has gone to the local public school or even the local private day school has never experienced a school community as strong as the community a boarding school provides; and this difference is important, because these are the people who are increasingly applying to us. The overwhelming majority of my students come from families which are first-generation private school, let alone boarding school. Our world is new to them, and thus our school culture with its strong identity and strong community is a new kind of school culture for parents used to the school "down the street."

When we speak to these parents about our schools and about how strong the feeling of community is on a boarding campus, we sometimes forget that this does not always make our schools appear attractive. The culture of the local day school is simply not as important as the culture of a boarding school. The culture of a day school remains dominated by the more important cultures of neighborhood and family. Thus, the culture of the local day school can usually be tolerated, ignored, or manipulated by parents at home if it is not a congenial one. Parents at day school influence their child on a daily basis and are usually part of a larger culture in their community or neighborhood which affects the school directly. Therefore, these day parents who went to day schools themselves are not always comfortable with the notion of a more powerful school culture.

Similarly, there is the largely emotional perception that they would be "giving up" their children, handing their children over to someone else to be raised. Of course, this is not what happens at all. Parents of boarding students remain in close contact with their child and their child's teachers and thus remain active participants in their child's education, even though they have chosen to take their child out of the local neighborhood and the local school and to place that child in a school away from home. In fact, most boarding parents would argue that they enjoy a better relationship with their child, because they sent their child to boarding school. Because they are no longer their child's study hall proctor in the evening and because they are no longer the social policeman on evenings and on weekends, they are able to establish a more positive relationship with their child at home and at school and also able to provide for their child's greater independence within the boundaries they have chosen.

Still, the reaction is an emotional one: "I would never send my child away." And the very fact that a parent is asked to send his or her child not just away from home but into a stronger community which will become itself a home away from home makes the decision for boarding all the more difficult to make. It is, in the end, a decision to broaden the circle of those who care for your child to include a school family: a deeper community where your child can live with friends and teachers, the better to learn and to grow up.

One of our mothers had a wonderful answer for her friends when they challenged her choice for boarding school. She would look them straight in the eye and insist on the truth: "Sending my child to boarding school was the hardest but also the most loving thing I could have ever done." She chose what was best for her child without denying it was difficult for her. She did not want her child to go away from home, but she wanted her child to live and learn in a stronger community, and she wanted her child to be taught and inspired by a stronger school culture, a culture which she herself had chosen.

And this, of course, is why most parents send their child to boarding school. The culture of the local day school does not "fit" their child's needs or their child's personality or their child's promise. The culture at home may not "fit" as well: both parents may work or travel a great deal; the parents may be divorced or separated or older; and this may be their only child at home. Similarly, the culture in the neighborhood may be the problem: no one goes to college, young people just "hang out" at the local mall. In any case, for whatever reason in any of the three cultures "at home," the parents need another choice, and this need for choice brings them to the boarding option.

For parents in search of a better fit for their child, boarding schools offer more choice, both in comparison to the local day school and in comparison to each other. Because we are boarding schools, drawing our students from a wider geographical area, we are able to develop and to maintain our own distinct identities. Like independent liberal arts colleges, we live by our reputations, building on our individual histories and traditions and seeking to enroll just the sort of student we think we can serve.

Thus, the decision to send your child to boarding school opens up a whole new kind of choice. No longer are you sending your child to a particular school because it is local or has the best academic reputation in your community or is the school which served your other children. You are sending your child to a school which you can choose especially for this particular person, seeking the best academic and social fit, and also seeking the community which lives by the same priorities, teaches the same values, and maintains the same standards as you do.

So here we are again, confronted with this extraordinary feeling of community which boarding schools alone can offer, each as a distinct society gathered around a particular identity and committed to a particular mission and culture. Surely, the opportunity to live and grow in such a community when it has been well chosen is a wonderful gift, a truly generous and loving one. Remember my student who thought nothing of coming to his headmaster's house to speak with him of his hopes and look ahead to the future; he is at home here; and being at home, he is well-taught and well-loved. Seek just this kind of fit for your child; broaden the circle, enlarge your home; but beware, all fine young people at good schools want to be teachers when they grow up.

A Sermon
at the Founders' Eucharist
on Parents' Weekend

*". . . he is like a man building a house, who dug deep,
and laid the foundation upon rock; and when a flood arose, the
stream broke against that house, and could not shake it, because
it had been well built."*
Luke 6:48

WHENEVER I SPEAK WITH ADMINISTRATORS AT OTHER SCHOOLS, I am struck by how different Saint James is from the schools where they administer, and thus by extension how different my own position as headmaster and chief administrator is in this remarkable community.

Because Saint James is a small school and a boarding school, and because I am not just a headmaster but also a priest, and because my house sits right in the middle of the campus, I tend to know the students a little better than most administrators.

I think back to the headmaster of the Harvard School in Los Angeles where I first taught. He administered a day school of some 650 boys. He knew a few of their names, but I would not even say that he knew most of them. Indeed, there were some students who went through the school without ever speaking to him. If you did not get into trouble or you did not win some sort of prize, there really was no reason to speak with the headmaster. On the whole, he counted on us to look after the students for him; he looked after the school.

And even as we cared for those students in that school, our job was problematic. In some cases we were able to establish close relationships, but in most cases, our relationships with our students were largely defined by an eight-to-three school day, and thus by the priorities of school life: teaching, coaching, college counseling; it was in these ways that we largely related to them. And, of course, this is how most schools operate; Saint James is very different.

And so, those of us who teach in this place, including me, the headmaster, tend to have a much closer relationship with our students, which is broader than the usual teacher student relationship. As teachers, we tend to parent a bit more than other teachers do, and thus find ourselves in a position more similar to our students' parents at home.

When I speak to a student about his work or about her behavior, I am very aware that I am not just addressing the presenting issue, but also often an underlying issue, usually an issue of relationship: the realtionship of that student with another student, that student with a particular teacher, that student with a parent or friend, sometimes, indeed, that student with me.

Because we live in a close community, we come to love each other in the right sense. We grow fond of each other, we come to rely upon each other, we come to feel connected in permanent and important ways which speak not just to the present but to the future, and not just to our relationships as teachers and students, but to our integrity as human beings.

And it is all played out (is it not?) in a healthy and constantly developing tension between our desire as adults to establish and deepen our relationships with these young people whom we care about and our obligation as teachers to play our role and to exercise our authority over them with fairness and compassion for their good.

And so, like parents, we find ourselves torn between our desire to bond with our students, to be open to them, available to them, to be with them, and our obligation to teach them and to direct them aright.

I will never forget my own experience two years ago when I made the mistake of trusting a group of students whom I should not have trusted; not because they were evil, they were not, but because I had not yet established a relationship with them of sufficient depth and sufficient strength that I could really trust them to honor their promises to me when these conflicted with the expectations of their friends.

And obviously a part of this story concerns their own integrity as young people growing up, but part of it also concerns my own integrity, my willingness as the adult in the parenting role to assume the proper authority even when it is not popular and to exercise it for the benefit of the young people I am appointed to serve.

And I remember that I got two messages from two different mothers on this occasion, both of them quite wise. One wrote "welcome to parenthood!", the other, "now you know why celibacy isn't so bad after all."

How many of you as parents hear the challenge "you don't trust me!" as "you don't love me?" How many of you fall for it? I did.

Allow a teacher who sometimes parents to reassure those of you who always parent: it's tough. It's tough to find that fine line between authority and bond which establishes the right parenting relationship. It's tough to make the unpopular decision, to test your child's loyalty, and to play "the heavy." Believe me, I know.

And yet, it is so essential that we do. It is so essential that we play our roles, be the adults, even if this means not being the best friend for one day or one week or 10 years. It is so essential that we hold our children accountable for their actions and help them to learn from their mistakes, even if this means that we need sometimes to stand back and watch them fall and not swoop in to save them.

In my brief experience as headmaster, I can think of two fathers: one who lied for his son, and one who did not; only one is a good father. I can think of two mothers: one who told her son to tell the truth and live with the consequences, and one who swooped in and blamed everybody else; only one is a good mother.

Show me a young man or a young woman with no character, and I will show you the parent who enabled it. It is sad to see.

But it is easy for me to cast stones. As I said, I am only sometimes with them; I am with them for a few months of a few years. You are always with them, as long as they have their own existence: you are their mothers and their fathers, and they will have no others.

And even though it is still frustrating for me to watch a student suffer in his or her moral development, because he or she has weak parents who lack the courage or the confidence to play their roles with authority, it is now at least more understandable, for I understand the temptation not to risk the bond; I am tempted too.

And I sometimes wonder if this is what Jesus meant when he spoke of temptation, the kind of temptation which good people face: the temptation to love in the wrong way, the temptation to answer our needs with the love of our children, rather than to answer their needs and to love them as God himself has shown us how to do.

For God's love as it is revealed to us in Jesus Christ is a love which does not seek to be fed but to feed, to be healed but to heal, to be forgiven but to forgive. It is a hard love which makes us accountable: it commissions us, empowers us, but never enables or enfeebles us; it is a generous love, a vigorous love, a brave love which does not count the cost in terms of popularity, only the victory in terms of what is true and good and lasting; it is moral, not just sentimental. It is the love revealed to us on the cross and the love revealed to us in this Eucharist. It is the foundation on which the wise man builds his house, a rock which is true and deep and solid.

So be not afraid: any house which is built upon this rock will stand, and any relationship which is built upon this love will live; it will live in the hearts of our children, and it will shine in the witness of their lives.

Amen.

A Sermon
At the Funeral of Richard Zellner,
Director of Food Service

*"[The Steward] hailed the bridegroom and said, 'Everyone
serves the best wine first, and waits until the guests have drunk
freely before serving the poorer sort; but you have kept the best
wine till now.' "*
John 2:10.

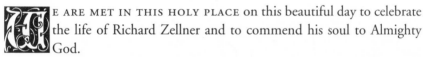E ARE MET IN THIS HOLY PLACE on this beautiful day to celebrate the life of Richard Zellner and to commend his soul to Almighty God.

As we all know and many of us know only too well, Rich's death has come to us as a great shock and a great tragedy. He was only 37 years old, and he leaves behind a wife much too young to be a widow and a son much too young to live without his father. He also leaves behind a whole host of co-workers and friends who shall miss him profoundly; and he leaves behind a whole community of students and teachers who really liked him and appreciated his good work and his good will on our behalf.

Thus, it is appropriate that we should be meeting here in the chapel, a place on his ground, his home, where he worked and lived and cared for us, where he left his mark, if you will, the last of many places in his short life which he made better by his presence.

And the question which is uppermost in many minds this day and brought, I am sure, to this place and to this altar is 'why?'.

Why should a man so young, still in the prime of his life, still needed by those around him, why should he die? Or even more to the point, why should a loving God have allowed this friend and husband and father to die so suddenly?

To answer the question directly is, I suppose, not much of a help to us just now. God gives each of us the freedom to live our lives and affect other people's lives as we choose. Certainly, Rich made choices in his life which in retrospect probably made his life shorter, but this was not his intention, and other people make similar choices and live for a very long time.

Rich, therefore, did not choose to die; rather, he chose to live, and he lived in his own way, as only he could live: full throttle, full energy all the time. This is who he was, and this was the nature of his presence with us; and if this is why he died so young, then this is also why we miss him, why his presence with us was so very important and so very substantial.

Perhaps the greatest help at a time like this is to recognize the great truth that God uses every human life as an occasion and every human being as an agent to bless and sustain His creation; or more to the point, in every life, God intends to love us. And so, each of us in our lives is given the opportunity to love those whom God has placed around us; this is the point of our lives, our purpose, the reason why we exist.

Rich was given this opportunity in his life, and it is to his great credit and our great benefit that he took this opportunity and lived his life for the people around him.

Therefore, the very fact that we miss him and wonder why he should have left us so suddenly and so quickly before we even had the opportunity to thank him reminds us and reassures us of God's good purpose for him and through him for us all.

The passage from the Gospel according to Saint John which we just heard read speaks to us on just this point.

Our Lord Jesus is at a wedding with his mother in Cana of Galilee. The bridegroom, who is the host of the party, has run out of wine, and the party is doomed. But Jesus, seeing the need, blesses six stone jars of water, creating new and better wine, blessing the marriage and the company. And Our Lord's agent in this is not the host; he perhaps does not even know that he has run out of wine. Rather, it is the steward, the one in charge of the feast, the one working to serve the gathering who acts as Our Lord's right hand. He is the one who first perceives the miracle and discovers the new wine, going to the bridegroom and telling him the good news: "Everyone serves the best wine first, and waits until the guests have drunk freely before serving the poorer sort; but you have kept the best wine till now."

For those of us who worked with him and knew him and relied upon him, this was Rich. He was the steward, the one who worked to build the company, the one who tended to the feast. And like the steward in this story, Rich was a good steward, the one who really cared, the one who wanted the party to go well, the one who never forgot the party's purpose: the people who were there.

Sonia and I were joking just last night that Rich had only one answer to anything I ever asked him: "No problem, Father." Now, let me commend this answer to the rest of the school; it would be wonderful if this was the only answer I ever received when I asked somebody to do something; I can assure you it is not. Still, in Rich's case, I honestly cannot remember any occasion on which he did not say "no problem," and, even better, did not mean it.

There was nothing Rich loved better than a party. All he had to do was hear a rumor that I was going to have one and he was up in my office ready to make it big. And as I look back on it, it really is very remarkable that the one who had to do the most work always looked forward to the party the most.

And it was not just parties for me, it was parties for everybody, especially the students. They were the ones Rich always cared about the most. He was always coming up with ideas: the soda machines, the pizza place, the vending machines, the salad bar, the yogurt machine, the snack bar; it just did not stop. As far as Rich was concerned, there was always something new to do, something that the kids would really love. Even the night before he died, he was planning a party for the Super Bowl; and he was very excited about it, looking forward to it, ready to go.

And in this way, by his enthusiasm and by his devotion to his work, Rich joined in the very purpose of God and acted faithfully as the agent for His miracles: miracles of hospitality and fellowship which built our community and made us stronger as a school and as a society.

When I spoke to the students in Chapel on Wednesday, I pointed out to them that Rich's life was especially admirable in three respects. First, he loved his work and never forgot what his work was for: the people he loved to serve. Secondly, he loved his wife with absolute devotion; he was proud of her, proud to be married to her; he adored her. Thirdly, he loved his son; he rejoiced in his talents and his goodness, and he looked to his future with pride and with confidence.

And all of this came together on a Saturday night at Saint James School in the dining hall, with Sonia and Robert and Rich and all of us: gummy worms and pizza and bad movies on the video, a wonderful place full of love and good will which was not there before him and will never be the same without him.

So you see, in the life of Rich Zellner, short as it was, God has loved us faithfully, for Rich was His true and faithful servant, the steward at the wedding feast, Christ's agent in the continuing miracle of His wonderful creation.

And so, may Christ the Son of God who sits at the right hand of the Father in heaven welcome our good friend to that feast of love which awaits us all, even the kingdom for which we pray. May He thank him on behalf of all of us for all that he has done for us, and may He welcome him as a guest to His party.

Amen.

A Sermon
Alumni Weekend

*"This is my commandment, that you love one another as
I have loved you."*
John 15:12

M R. COLLIN, the Chairman of our English Department and Drama
Teacher, has often told me how he feels for the clergy at Saint James:
"It must be really difficult to stand up there in Chapel every morning
and say the same thing. How many different ways can you say, 'God is love?'

Now, every time he says this (and he says this often), I take his point.
There is a simplicity to the Christian understanding of God (and thus, the
Christian understanding of life) which can seem monotonous: we believe that
God is love; it is in fact that simple.

Which is to say that all that we should live for, all that we should attempt
to do with our lives, is determined by that one revelation of God in Jesus
Christ, that one understanding of what life is about, that one great purpose of
love which created us, redeems us, and alone can bring us joy.

In the passage from St. John's Gospel which we just heard, Jesus presents
himself as the vine, and he challenges us to be His branches, so that the creative purpose of life revealed in him may be revealed in us. And as we consider
His image, we do better I think to think of a vine in spring, barren wood
bursting suddenly and bursting forcefully into leaf and into flower.

For Christ reveals to us the very life of God which is dynamic, that love
of God which reaches out into the world and gives our lives their meaning.
And He invites us to join in that love, as branches to His vine, indistinguish-
able, lost in the foliage, bearing fruit, fruit that will last, God's fruit, God's
good deeds by us and through us in His world.

And so, this purpose of love which Christ reveals to us is meant to live in us, to inspire us and empower us to care about other people, to offer ourselves for them in God's way, which is the way of life. And this way of life is remarkable; it is different from our own; not the way which any of us would choose and certainly not the way which others often choose around us.

But this of course is His point when he says to us quite frankly, "You did not choose me, but I chose you and appointed you that you should go and bear fruit and that your fruit should abide." There is in the end only one good way for us to live our lives, and Christ has shown it.

Christ has shown us this way by his remarkable and strange teaching that we should turn the other cheek, walk the extra mile, give all that we have and all that we own, that we might love our neighbor as ourself. He has shown us this way by his miracles of hospitality, healing, and forgiveness; and He has shown us this way by His own good example of perfect love, His faithful willingness to suffer and to die rather than to inflict suffering and to cause death.

But Christ did not just reveal the love of God in his own life of extraordinary faithfulness and sacrifice, He also found love and pointed to love as He found that love already present and active in the world.

With His presence and first miracle at Cana in Galilee, Christ blessed the pre-existing custom of marriage and held it up as a sign to us of the kind of faithful and generous love which can make our human lives shine with God's own purpose.

As a teacher, he cared for his disciples and sought to teach them the truth, no matter how hard the lesson or how challenging the concept, he sought to teach them: "the truth in love," as Saint Paul describes it.

As a son, He loved His mother and received her love for Him with reverence and with gratitude; He honored her and cared for her even as He hung on the Cross, commending her to His friend and commending His friend to His mother that she would not be left alone.

And He had friends, real friends, deep friends, true friends, friends who angered Him and disappointed Him yes, but still the friends whom He forgave, friends He loved, not just liked, but loved; and they loved Him. Peter and John, Mary and Martha were jealous for His attention. Mary Magdalen grieved for Him. They sought to find with Him that intimacy which only friends can find: They were eager to be with Him, to know Him, to understand Him, to help Him, and to protect Him, even from His own good purpose.

And He loved them for this: He wept for them, and asked for them, and sought them out, especially after His Resurrection when His love for them was even more intimate and more demanding: "Peter, do you love me? Do you love me more than these?" "Yes, Lord, you know that I love you."

And so finally, in this passage, Our Lord points to His friendships proudly and speaks of them as invitations to discipleship, revealing the love of God which He Himself reveals: "Greater love has no man than this, that a man lay down his life for his friends. You are my friends if you do what I command you. No longer do I call you servants, for the servant does not know what his master is doing; but I have called you friends, for all that I have heard from my Father I have made known to you."

Thus, we as the friends of Christ can understand the purpose of Christ and join in His purpose to reveal His glory to the world.

So what was it? What was it in life that Our Lord found to bless and to redeem? What did he see already here with us, already here in our lives together which he could point to and say, "Yes, this is what your lives are meant to be about; build on this, grow on this, work with this, keep going; 'I am the vine and you are the branches.' "

What did he find to bless?

He found this: He found the love of man and wife in marriage, the love of parent and child, teacher and student, friends in friendship; and He blessed this love. He blessed it, and he said keep going, grow from here: "This is my commandment, that you love one another as I have loved you."

And I ask you, is this not the place for this? Is this not the place where just this miracle has happened and happens all around us?

Surely this is why those of you who are alumni have come back this weekend? You remember this place as the place where it happened, where it began, where life itself confronted you, took hold of you, and called you on your journey?

And you remember those who were with you here: your friends and your teachers, the ones you loved as they loved you. For this is where you learned to love, to give as well as to receive.

And some of you saw this even as you were here at school, some saw it just as you were leaving, most probably saw it after you were gone: this place for you was holy; Christ Himself was rooted here, and you became his branches.

And alas, of course, there are some who are not here who will never see it; because they are too angry or too selfish or really just too immature, because they have yet to grow; they simply do not want to see it here or anywhere else where they have lived; and God as Love will never force them to see it.

But no matter who sees it, the love which grows here and finds its life here is real and true and lasting; it is something which is here just waiting to be recognized, waiting to be noticed. It is sacred; and like all sacred things, it is difficult for us to describe or even fully to appreciate, because it comes from God. It happens through us and for us and in spite of us; it uses us, redeems us, and brings us home at last to heaven.

And so in this way, the vine is rooted here and it grows, from this hill and from this spring where it was planted by those good men so long ago. It grows forcefully and quietly, sometimes lush and sometimes spartan, but always alive, always pushing out its branches, green with new life, full of foliage: reaching up and out into the world beyond this place where the fruit it bears must ripen.

Amen.

AN ESSAY

"For the sake of the students whom we are dedicated to serve:"
Howard Gardner's Theory of Multiple Intelligences
and the Practice of Saint James School

NE OF OUR TRUSTEES, John Henry '67, had occasion to meet Professor Howard Gardner at Harvard and was impressed by how much his theory of Multiple Intelligences pertained to our work at Saint James. As some of you may remember, I referred to this theory in several talks I gave while we were renovating the Cotton Building as the Bowman-Byron Fine Arts Center because I was stressing the importance of the arts in our curriculum. Now that we are proceeding to a new capital campaign to strengthen and assure our future as a small coeducational boarding school, it seems timely to me to refer to Professor Gardner's theory again.

Gardner's theory has much broader implications for our work than our need for an arts center, however; it serves, I think, as a very powerful apology for much of what we seek to do as a school and indeed much of what distinguishes us from other schools. In its light, we have done well to retain our familial character as a small, boarding community, to continue to balance the academic success of our students with their successes outside the classroom, and to remain primarily focused on our students' personal and ethical development. Indeed, if we accept Gardner's broader understanding of human intelligence and share his concern that schools teach students with different abilities more effectively, then Saint James offers some healthy challenges to the prevailing model of American secondary education.

A small but diverse boarding school with a clear moral focus and challenging expectations for student behavior stands apart from the more typical larger day school with its eight-to-three school day and local student body. The issues we seek to address at school are the issues most schools leave unaddressed, the relationships we seek to establish between students and between students and their teachers are more substantial and more demanding than those established in most school communities. The result, of course, is a stronger emphasis on personal growth and moral development and a higher valuation of those traits of character and personality in our students which we consider to be admirable and worth developing.

I apologize for the length of this essay, but Professor Gardner's theory is a provocative and a far-reaching one, especially as it applies to Saint James. I apologize also to Professor Gardner, as I am sure that I have done his theory little justice; I commend to you his book, *Frames of Mind: The Theory of Multiple Intelligences* (Harper Collins, 1993).

As I gather my thoughts, I am mindful of the fact that I have now served four years as headmaster, and I am very aware of the many students now graduated and those still with us whom I have known to benefit from the community which I describe. Those who know me well, know that I am tempted to tell many anecdotes to illustrate the points which I am making here, but I resist. Suffice it to say that there are many faces that go with these thoughts and the experiences which have produced them; they smile before me in my mind as I write, and I could not be more proud of them.

GARDNER'S THEORY AND SECONDARY
EDUCATION GENERALLY

In his theory of multiple intelligences, Howard Gardner argues that we have seven major intelligences which can be distinguished and described as linguistic, musical, logical-mathematical, spatial, bodily-kinesthetic, intrapersonal, and interpersonal. As it has developed, the academic curriculum in secondary schools tends to focus on only two of these intelligences: linguistic and mathematical-logical. These are the intelligences most involved in the study of the five standard subjects of English, history, foreign language, math, and science, and these are the intelligences tested in the SAT. The reason for this is obvious: these are the intelligences which we have come to value as most important in quantifying a student's ability to perform successfully in university and in the professions beyond.

By placing these two "academic" intelligences within the wider context of seven distinguishable intelligences, Gardner makes the valuable argument that our present system has become too narrow, forcing us to undervalue the general intelligence of students who are in fact gifted in the five other areas. Further, students who have a primary intelligence outside the two academic intelligences often find school to be a boring, even stifling place where others' gifts are valued and theirs are not, and thus a place rigged against them where they are doomed to failure and see no reason to succeed. This is particularly true in the typical American high school where students are almost always encouraged to distinguish themselves from each other as they develop their strengths. Thus, we have the strong school cultural distinctions between "jocks" and "nerds," students who are good in science and students who are good in English, the football hero and the star on stage. Of course, there are also those students who are not really stars in anything—"nice kids," good "all-rounders," who obey the rules and do well enough, but never particularly shine because they are never particularly engaged; these, to my mind, are the most compelling.

In our advocacy of the arts and athletics as essential parts of any good secondary school curriculum, educators generally have long recognized the importance of those intelligences which Gardner defines as "spatial," "musical," and "bodily-kinesthetic." We have perhaps relegated these intelligences a little too firmly to the side of the academic day, and thus failed to recognize and employ them as effectively as we might within the classroom; but we have nonetheless continued to recognize athletic, musical, and artistic achievement within the wider context of our school communities. Nonetheless, recent growth in the size of secondary schools and greater parental pressure for students to excel have caused schools to fission and departmentalize; just as the history teacher has very little to do with the football coach these days, so the history student has very little to do with the football player; they are different folk. Students who are challenged in the classroom, avoid challenging subjects and challenging teachers; similarly, students who are challenged in sports, choose P.E. and other non-physical activities. And because of this, each student loses the experience of working with the other and thus the opportunity of working together with someone who is more challenged or less challenged in that particular activity or discipline.

To my mind, the most compelling part of Gardner's theory is his definition of the two personal intelligences: intrapersonal and interpersonal. Gardner defines intrapersonal intelligence as our developing "sense of self" and interpersonal intelligence as our developing sense of other people. Of all the seven intelligences, these are the most important, because they establish our own ability as individuals to be happy and productive in our lives. We have all witnessed the phenomenon of the C+ student who goes on to be supremely successful in a chosen field or again the phenomenon of the lousy athlete never chosen for the team who goes on to be a courageous and effective leader. We find in each case a strong individual with a good sense of self and a good sense of how to work with other people, a remarkable person if you will, someone with strong personal intelligences unrecognized and undervalued when he or she was in school.

The problem, of course, is that it is difficult to know how a school can recognize and value these personal intelligences, because they are hard to perceive objectively and thus to quantify. The students with linguistic intelligence will employ the greater vocabulary and write the better essays; the students with mathematical-logical intelligence will solve the problems and earn the perfect scores; the students with bodily-kinesthetic intelligence will make the baskets and win the games; but the students with personal intelligence will find their successes in their relationships with other people, both those with whom they interrelate as peers and those with whom they interrelate as figures in authority. Essays can be graded and tests can be scored and games can be won, but relationships are difficult to judge and to recognize, and thus to value. This is particularly true when relationships are developed within the constraints of an eight-to-three school day, a 45-minute period with some 30 students in the classroom.

And yet, as Gardner argues, adolescence remains an absolutely vital time for the development of these personal intelligences, the time when we learn who we are and learn to deal effectively, as ourselves, with other people: "We see, then, during the turbulent years of adolescence, a maturation of knowledge of one's own person as well as of knowledge of other persons. But at the same time, within many cultures, an even more crucial event is taking place. Adolescence turns out to be that period of life in which individuals must bring together these two forms of personal knowledge into a larger and more organized sense, a sense of identity or . . . a sense of self." (*Frames of Mind*, p. 251) For schools to ignore these personal intelligences and to fail to identify, challenge, and value them in our students so that they can be elicited and developed is to undervalue and thus to stymie students of remarkable character capable of great achievement who are in fact the very students whom schools should be identifying and encouraging to be leaders for our future.

SAINT JAMES SCHOOL

Like all American secondary schools with a college preparatory curriculum, Saint James continues to challenge and to develop the linguistic and logical-mathematical intelligences primarily in a core curriculum of English, history, foreign language, math, and science. Bodily-kinesthetic intelligence is primarily developed in the athletic program which is mandatory in all three seasons; but it is also developed in the drama program, which is voluntary but active, the students producing six plays just this last year. Spatial intelligence is developed in sports and in certain academic subjects such as geometry and physics, but primarily in studio art, which is required in the middle school and a popular elective in the upper; also in chess club, stage crew, and the yearbook, which are popular student activities. Finally, musical intelligence is developed every morning in chapel where we always sing and listen to music. There is an active chapel choir and a staged musical in the spring, electives in music, and opportunities for instrumental instruction and performance. Again, there is a required music program in the middle school. During the course of the year, there are several musical and dramatic performances staged in the auditorium, which everyone attends; further, there is a Fine Arts requirement that all students attend artistic performances if they are not involved in the arts actively.

Certainly, the five non-personal intelligences have been departmentalized at Saint James much as they would be at any other college preparatory school with a traditional academic curriculum. It is difficult to see how this can be avoided; further, given the premium which our culture places upon linguistic and mathematical-logical intelligences in the academic disciplines, it is questionable whether we would want to. Indeed, as regards linguistic intelligence, Saint James is a particularly challenging school, taking advantage of small class sizes and a student-teacher ratio of 7:1 to require frequent and substantial writing assignments in history and English. Teachers encourage students to submit rough drafts and often work with students during free periods and in the evenings to review their rough drafts and help them to prepare their essays.

Even though Saint James retains the traditional distinction between academic and extracurricular activities, and thus runs the risk of undervaluing the non-academic intelligences, we require extracurricular participation and value extracurricular achievement, and this maintains a balance. In this regard, we are helped by two essential characteristics:

First, as a small school, we can require participation, and in fact need participation, in all of our extracurricular activities. Given our size, if we did not require athletics, we could not field teams; and our teams need the participation of every student interested. Because of this need, the student who would not participate in a sport at a larger school will participate with us, and thus meet new challenges and find new talents in a different context. Similarly, the student who otherwise would not sing, sings; the student who otherwise would not act, acts; and so forth. Further, the good student is placed on the field with the good athlete, and the good athlete in the class with the good student; each is given the opportunity to appreciate the strengths and help address the weaknesses of the other.

Second, as a boarding school, Saint James can schedule a full day with classes in the morning, sports in the afternoon, choir rehearsal in the evening, and a full week with games on Saturdays and events on weekends. This means that a dedicated student can be an active athlete and play the lead in the school play, because this student is not forced to choose between two activities scheduled for the same time period. Further, students living in the dormitories have the opportunity to develop friendships beyond the usual boundaries that divide other high school students and then to be drawn by those friendships into new areas of appreciation, challenge, and reward.

It is in the area of personal intelligences, however, that Saint James particularly stands apart. Again, because Saint James is a small school and a boarding school, students are required to inter-relate in several contexts: socially during their free time in the common areas and in the dormitories, academically in the classroom and outside the classroom as they help each other with their work, athletically on teams as they compete with a mixed group of athletes against teams from larger schools, and extracurricularly as they join with other students in common interests and common projects. In this way, students at Saint James are encouraged to cross the boundaries that would divide them in larger schools, make friendships with students who have different primary intelligences than they do, and learn to succeed where they are challenged and to be helpful where they are gifted. Thus, the good student tutors his friend in chemistry, even as his friend teaches him how to cradle a lacrosse ball; the stands are full at sports events, and the seats are filled at plays, as students attend to support their friends.

There is one other characteristic of Saint James which helps to make this interaction between students particularly educational and challenging: diversity.

Again, because Saint James is a boarding school, we enroll students from all over the country and all over the world, representing the full range of racial, religious, and socio-economic backgrounds. Further, as a coeducational school, we educate young men and women in school together, each with their own dormitories and athletic programs, but all of them on campus, in the classroom, the dining hall, and in school activities together. This is perhaps the greatest challenge of all, the challenge which young women and young men face in today's America: to relate well to each other socially as friends and neighbors, professionally as coworkers and colleagues, and not just romantically as boyfriend and girlfriend.

And yet, as I consider this issue of personal intelligence and our community here at school, Saint James stands apart the most in the quality of those interrelationships which develop between our students and our teachers. Again, because we are a small school and a boarding school, Saint James provides and encourages relationships between students and teachers which are both close and genuine. Students at larger boarding schools are often able to avoid these relationships and relate simply with their peers, and students at day schools even more so; but boarders and faculty in a small community on the same campus together cannot avoid each other for long. Thus, students are not only challenged to develop good relationships with their peers on an interpersonal level, but also with their teachers who are adults in authority over them. The Latin master might also be the dorm master and the cross-country coach; the drama coach might also be the English master and the weekend duty captain. These are not figures to be treated lightly, lied to, or ignored; rather, these are important figures in the boarders' lives requiring attention, respect, and understanding. Similarly, the student on the hall is not just someone else's problem at three o'clock, rather the student is ours, requiring our attention and our compassion.

And here, it is important to note that it is exactly these strong relationships between students and between students and their teachers which often inspire our students to achieve beyond even their own expectations in their classes, in the arts, or in athletics. In our community together and with the real human relationships which this community sustains, we can appeal to those students whose primary intelligences are personal to develop their other intelligences as well. Indeed, if I were to select a type of student whom I think we serve especially well, I would select this type; these are the ones who succeed at Saint James better than they would succeed somewhere else. Further, what is true about the influence of the personal intelligences upon the other intelligences holds true for the influence of the personal intelligences upon each other: those students with a strong sense of self are challenged by our community to develop a more compassionate and honest concern for everyone else, and those students with a strong concern for everyone else are challenged to develop a stronger sense of who they are themselves and thus their own ability to stand against the crowd as their sense of self requires.

Finally, again because we are a small boarding school and live in community together, we hold our students accountable to a higher standard of behavior and morality. Thus, the student who risks smoking marijuana on campus, risks being caught with the inevitable consequence of dismissal. Similarly, the student who has been chosen to act as a prefect and assumes this position of real leadership and trust is held accountable to the higher standard which this position requires; it is no longer acceptable for this student to bend the rules for a friend or to set the wrong example; it is corrupt. This is why prefects are only appointed if they are nominated by both the faculty and the students; both relationships are important. The successful prefect needs the personal strength to relate honestly and appropriately to peers and to teachers alike.

These are hard, genuine challenges for young people to assume, especially as they answer to adults other than their parents. As we all know, teachers and parents are different in that parents can assume the subjective view when teachers often cannot. Issues of fairness in the school and concern for other students require that the rules be enforced justly, and individual students who make the wrong decisions must expect to suffer the same consequences as anybody else. Still, occasions for students to learn who they are and how they should behave in situations of real risk and real temptation provide opportunities for personal reflection and growth well beyond anything experienced in the more limited setting of a day school. In short, the challenge is greater, but so is the reward. And thus, it is especially appropriate that the school's highest prize, the Bishop's Prize, is not an academic or an athletic prize, rather a character prize, given by vote of the faculty to that Sixth Former who "by leadership and personal example has done the most for Saint James School." It is given to that Sixth Former who has shown the highest level of personal intelligence in his or her engagement with our community, who has met the challenge and grown in response.

CONCLUSION

What Saint James offers, therefore, is the example of a secondary school which values all seven intelligences in our students and seeks to develop these intelligences in our students as they learn and grow at school. Further, of these seven intelligences, Saint James values the personal intelligences most and seeks to develop in our students a strong sense of who they are and how they should relate to others in their lives. Several characteristics of the school are essential to this mission: that we should be a boarding school where the days and weeks are long and students and teachers can live in community together; that we should be a small school where all the students can know each other and work together for achievement in the several aspects of our common life; that we should be a diverse school where all the students can live and learn together with students with many different talents and many different challenges, students of both sexes, from all over the world and country, from every race, religion, and socio-economic background; and that we should be a morally demanding school with high expectations for our students' behavior and conduct, where students will be held accountable to real rules with real consequences, and be given substantial opportunities to exercise effective responsibility for good in our community.

Finally, there is one additional characteristic of Saint James which stands out as the source of all that we have done from our beginning, the reason why we seek to educate the whole person and not just the student and why we value the character of that person more than any gift or talent or ability. We are a church school, founded by the Episcopal Church in America in the longer tradition of the great "public" schools in England. In this tradition, we have always stressed the essential interrelationship of body, mind, and spirit, and valued each as important in the education of our students. Further, we have always considered the character of our students, their will and their personality to be the overriding, defining element of their personhood. As we have sought to educate their minds, we have also sought to educate their souls, to encourage and strengthen within them that proper sense of identity and true purpose, which Gardner calls a developed sense of self.

For us, then, Gardner's theory is not quite new; it is, rather, a restating of the classical, believing humanist approach to education which inspired the reform of the English "public" schools in the nineteenth century and inspired our own founding in 1842. Dr. Arnold at Rugby and Dr. Kerfoot at Saint James both would have agreed wholeheartedly that we should educate the whole person whom we teach and encourage our students to be good. Still, Gardner's theory is new in the sense that he calls gifts of talent and of character "intelligences," using the same word which we once reserved exclusively for gifts of reason and of language. In this way, he re-emphasizes the importance of the non-academic intelligences and reminds us of our opportunity to value these more appropriately and thus to appreciate the whole spectrum of our students' abilities. By appealing to their strengths, we can develop their weaknesses, and by addressing their weaknesses, we can develop their strengths; but all of this, we can only achieve by continuing to strengthen our received, distinct character as Saint James: a small boarding school with a diverse student body and a challenging expectation for student behavior and conduct. As Saint James, we have this opportunity for our future, and we must seize it for the sake of the students whom we are dedicated to serve.

An Essay
My Vision of a School Library:
Mission Control for Learning

Written for the National Association for Independent
School Librarians

AINT JAMES SCHOOL NEEDS A NEW LIBRARY. Though busy and functioning and full of life, our present library is too small and bursting at the seams. We need more shelving space and floor space, and we need to make more of a statement than our present space affords. And so, our present need places before me as the headmaster my usual task of raising money, eliciting the support to build something new.

All of which begs some questions: what kind of library do we want? what is it that I will approach our friends to ask for? why do we need something new? and what is it that we need?

Knowing that I have grappled with these questions over the past several years, Mark Hillsamer, who is still the librarian at the school where I was a student, asked me to offer my present thoughts for this publication, to describe to you who are school librarians just what it is that this head of school is looking for in his school's new library.

Now obviously my vision for a library reflects something of the particular character of Saint James School as well as my own academic history and prejudices. In fact, as I consider it, I am probably most inspired by my seven years in Oxford and the way in which the college libraries operated in the two colleges to which I belonged. Still, I think that there is a list of characteristics I am looking for in our new library which are not particular to Saint James or even to me and which I can perhaps offer in a general outline of what all of us should be looking for as we plan and administer our own libraries, each of us in our own schools.

I offer first a list of what a school library should be:

1) *It should be a place for study* where students in small groups and students individually can engage in academic work: do their assigned reading, write their essays, and prepare for tests.

2) *It should be a place for research* where students can use the resources of the library both on shelves and through computers to answer the questions and prepare the topics assigned to them by their teachers.

3) *It should be a place for literary relaxation and recreation* where students can browse through open shelves and read quietly in corners, pursuing their own interests, developing their own dreams, and indulging their own fantasies.

4) *It should be a place for faculty as well as students* where teachers can prepare in their subjects and pursue their own research and interests. The teachers' day is busy, so the library needs to serve them as a present and a reliable resource.

5) *It should be a place for learning* which proclaims by its presence and by its quality the priorities of the institution it serves. In this role, the library represents the academic priority for the school in the same way that a large gymnasium or an indoor swimming pool represent the athletic priority or a beautiful chapel the spiritual priority. Where does the school place its resources? What spaces make significant statements on campus? What are the centers of its life?

6) *It should be a place of permanence for the whole community* which provides resources and makes a statement beyond any one teacher or any one discipline or even beyond the present generation of students to those who came before and those who will come after; it is a place for alumni to return to see where they were students, again like the court where they once played basketball or the chapel where they once prayed; it is a place where they can see their friends in their memories, still sitting with them at that table by the window or in those chairs by the door.

Now that I have spoken positively about what a school library should be, let me say what it should not be:

1) *It should not be a study hall* with imposed silence, seat assignments, and a rigid, censorious discipline; it is a freer, busier, slightly noisier place than that.

2) *It should not be a computer lab* where books are rejected as obsolete and not quite "modern;" *neither should it be a fortress for books* where computers

are rejected as noisy and "not quite real." It should be a place for research where computers are running and books flow in and out to pause again on tables with articles on screens: information moves in this place into minds and onto essays; eyes glide down pages, pens write on paper, and fingers race on keys.

3) *It should not be a student center* where students grab a bite, drink their sodas, and lounge on sofas, shouting to friends across the room; it should be a studious place; its purpose is more serious and its atmosphere is more solemn.

4) *It should not be a faculty lounge* where students may be seen but not heard, and teachers gather to discuss their students and each other over coffee; it should be a shared space for students and for faculty alike; they have this place in common; they are scholars here together.

5) *It should not be a front parlor which rarely gets used* and then only by the headmaster for alumni cocktail parties and the admissions director for applicant tours: "look at our beautiful library, see how elegant it is, how quiet and how empty."

6) *It should not be a museum or a mausoleum*; it should be permanent, but not frozen, grand but not intimidating, elegant but functional; it needs to make the right statement, but it should function as this statement: it should be alive with discovery and busy with new study.

Certainly, we live in changing times. Computerization and developing technologies are providing us with new opportunities to increase the information our libraries can provide while at the same time helping us to contain their size and cost. Changes in teaching styles and more interactive learning strategies are affecting the way students work in our libraries as places for study; the days of libraries dedicated solely to students working silently and independently with book and pen on paper are over. The atmosphere in our libraries has changed, just as the atmosphere in our schools has changed around them: they are livelier and busier, more multifaceted in their services and activities. Still, they remain dedicated to the same essential academic purpose, and thus remain empowered to provide for our schools the same strong academic statement and resources.

Therefore, as we continue to engage with these changes, it remains essential that we as heads and librarians work closely together to maintain the library's central role in our schools, and that we continue to defend and advocate the library as "mission control" for learning.

Fall 1996

A SERMON
AT THE PARENTS' WEEKEND EUCHARIST

"For it will be as when a man going on a journey called
his servants and entrusted to them his property; to one he gave
five talents, to another two, to another one, to each according
to his ability."
Matthew 25:14

THIS PAST SUMMER I made the mistake of going on vacation with my computer. Those of you who travelled in July to New England as I did will recall that it rained a lot, and thus I found myself with the time and the occasion to do some reading, to reflect upon four good years at Saint James, and even to order some of my thoughts in an essay which you should have received in the mail.

In this essay, I attempted something of a dialogue with Howard Gardner, using his theory of multiple intelligences to explain the ways we teach at Saint James. Those of you who found a chance to read this article, or better yet a chance to read Gardner's actual book on the subject, will recall that Gardner argues that all of us are gifted with several different "intelligences," not just the two academic intelligences of mathematical-logical and linguistic reasoning, but also musical, spatial, and bodily-kinesthetic "intelligences," as well as intrapersonal and interpersonal "intelligences" which allow us to develop a strong sense of ourselves and to relate effectively as ourselves to other people in our lives.

As I pointed out in my essay, Gardner's theory is not so much "new" as a new assertion of an almost obvious truth: there are many gifts which God can give to us as talents for our lives, and each of us is given our own distinctive mix. Thus, not every one of us is gifted as an athlete or gifted as a musician or gifted as an artist, just as not everyone of us is gifted as a student in math and science or in English and history. We all have our own gifts, our own resources to bring to the challenges and opportunities of life.

In the parable which I have chosen from St. Matthew's Gospel, Jesus makes something of the same point. A man of property leaves on a journey, and he leaves behind a sum of money to be invested by three servants: the first receives five talents, the second receives two talents, and the third receives one talent. Each of the first two servants invests his talents wisely and receives two-fold on his investment; so upon his return, the master is pleased. The third servant simply hides his talent by burying it in the ground, thus he fails to make a profit, and the master is disappointed.

Clearly, with this parable, Jesus is reminding us that we are all different and that each of us is given unique gifts to invest for the Kingdom of Heaven. Just as the master entrusts each servant with a certain sum of money, so each of us is entrusted by God with a certain sum of gifts and advantages in life with which we are empowered to build and to create for God's purpose in the world.

By making this point in a parable, Jesus leaves open to us just what these gifts and talents might be. Certainly, we have Gardner's list of "intelligences," different abilities to engage effectively with our existence: the abilities to engage musically, spatially, bodily, logically, linguistically, and personally; gifts of talent and reason, of personality and character. But we also have additional gifts which distinguish us even further: what we look like, the material and social advantages which our parents are able to give to us, the country where we are born, the time in which we live, who happens to teach us, who happens to befriend us, in all these ways we are "gifted," each of us differently, and thus each of us set apart.

Only consider what it means to be born in a country at peace, to be born in America and not in Bosnia, or rather even in the suburbs of Washington and not in the inner city: the gift of peace which we take so much for granted, let alone the further gifts of health and wealth, privilege and talent.

And this, of course, is part of what Jesus is saying: this "gifting" to us by God, this entrusting us with talents; it does not seem quite fair.

Right away when we hear this parable, we are struck by the fact that each servant receives a different amount of talents: one receives five, the other two, the last only one.

If all of us think back to our experience of growing up, we will recall that constant humiliating revelation that we were not given as much as other people were, especially as we sought to compete against them.

I always remember that horrible, mortifying moment when they were picking teams in soccer, and I was always one of the last to be chosen, or that friend who never needed to memorize anything for the Latin test, because he always just knew it; the girl in the piano recital who really could play the piano; the boy at school whose father was famous. The list goes on: the popular student in kindergarten whose choice of valentines and whose guest list for birthday parties determined who was elect and who was damned; the baseball player in seventh grade who never dropped a catch and always hit home runs; the math wiz in eleventh grade who always understood the formula and could correct the teacher at the board. How I wanted to be one of these, but I was not.

So, in that moment of profound envy and humiliation, we feel, each of us, that we have just the one talent, the boy on the right has two, and the girl on the left has five. God is not fair.

But Jesus does not offer us any particular answer to this question of fairness, and this is wise on his part; because we would not listen to Him anyway, anymore than we listened to our mothers and our fathers when they tried to remind us of our own particular talents: "look how gifted you are in this area or that area." "Yes, but he or she is better." There is always at least one of them, often more; and God usually places them right in front of us in the race where we can see them running on ahead of us or right next to us in class where we can hear them respond with the right answer. "How does he do that? How does she know that? Why can't I?"

It is, of course, one of the greatest ironies of life and indeed one of the greatest causes of sadness in life that none of us is ever able to really appreciate his or her own particular blessings. Even those who appear to appreciate their talents and their advantages, dazzling and intimidating us with self-promoting tales of personal greatness, are themselves actually vain and idle in their boasting, in fact even more insecure than we are.

No, Jesus in his gentleness does not overwhelm us with the truth about us as it can be seen by God, rather he accepts our human weakness, adopting our perspective and showing us the answer to our predicament. He reminds us that what others have does not matter to us, rather what matters to us is what we have; these are the talents which God himself has given us, and only fear can hold us back.

The servant with the one talent is not condemned by the master because he receives one talent, rather he is condemned because he fails to invest this talent and to build upon it boldly. And he fails, of course, because he is afraid: "Master, I knew you to be a hard man, reaping where you did not sow, and gathering where you did not winnow; so I was afraid, and I went and hid your talent in the ground."

Here is the point, the whole point of the parable: let us not be afraid. Let us not look around and see what everybody else has and decide that we do not have enough; let us rather look to what we have and try as ourselves with these gifts. Maybe we are not God's gift to baseball, but we can try to catch and hit the ball; and in trying, we may well prove to be God's gift to the team. Maybe we are not God's gift to mathematics, maybe even not God's gift to walking up the stairs, but we are nonetheless God's gift: unique, valuable, and chosen. By our very effort, our very ability to redeem the challenges placed before us, we shine with the purpose of our Creator, and we reveal His purpose to those who know us best and thus know just how we have struggled: those who love us best; our friends, our family, and our teachers.

The most wonderful feeling a teacher can have is a feeling we experience often at Saint James, perhaps even more often because it is Saint James; it is the joy we feel as teachers when a particular student achieves beyond his or her talent and shows in that achievement a kind of triumph of spirit and victory of purpose which is truly humbling to behold.

I know that I am pleased when the gifted history student does well in my European history class and does well on the Advanced Placement Examination; but I rejoice in my heart when the student who is more challenged succeeds beyond our common expectation.

If you will allow me, to witness such a victory, however small, is to live for a moment in the love of God, to see revealed God's own creative purpose, to rejoice with the master in the triumph of his servant. Maybe it was five talents, maybe it was two, maybe it was one; who cares? The gift has doubled.

And I know that I am not alone in this feeling. The whole school feels this when a team does particularly well in a difficult match or contest, winning with grit and with spirit against the odds. The team feels this when a particular player, not necessarily the best player, plays his or her heart out, shaming the others to join in the effort, hopeless as it may seem, leaving fear behind.

This is what I found in this place when I came here, and this is what I want to preserve and to encourage in this place. I want Saint James to remain a place where students are encouraged to build upon their talents as each of them may have them, and also to remain a place where they help each other in the common enterprise of learning, encouraging each other and learning from each other as they reach within themselves to find in their hearts that one essential talent which is all that any of us will ever need: that spirit of life and for life which God Himself has given us, that spirit of love to inspire and to redeem us all.

Amen.

A Letter
To the Editors of the
Washington Post

Dear Sirs,

I write to thank David Ignatius for his excellent article in praise of Canon Martin.

Like many, indeed most of Canon Martin's boys, I would say that his influence upon me has been immeasurable. He is without doubt one of the heroes of my childhood, a rock at the foundation of my adolescent universe whose personal example of permanence, discipline, and integrity caught my attention and focused my ambition growing up.

Even now that I am no longer one of his "boys," a bit older and a bit further on that journey he once walked with me, I hear his words in my own, and I see his challenge especially now before me, because I am for others what he was for me: a priest and a headmaster.

And so, after I read David's essay in this morning's paper, I walked up the hill from my house to the Saint James School Chapel, there to speak to the young as he once spoke to us; for it is, after all, Monday morning.

And what could I tell them, but what he told us? "Choose the hard right against the easy wrong." What can I tell them about life, but that "this is the first day of the rest of it?" About challenge, but that "it is good?" About failure, but that it comes to us as "a gift to test our worth?" And how can I even begin to speak about love as substantially and as generously as he did? How can I teach them as he taught us that the world is wonderful before us and that each of us has the opportunity to grow in grace towards God, to love our neighbor as ourself, to make real and immediate that Kingdom of God for which we pray?

The word "love" arrests me, and this is what I tell them: we loved the man, and he loved us. We knew that when Canon Martin spoke to us in chapel as a group or in person in the hallways, at his table, or in his study, that he cared for us and that he prayed for us. We knew that our selfishness distressed him, our need to boast annoyed him, our willingness to quit appalled him; but we also knew that our ability to achieve and our eagerness to learn inspired his life.

There is, in the end, that one question in life which love demands of us; I hear it in his voice to this day: "By gosh, Dunnan, are you being good?" I hope he knows that I try.

Yours faithfully,

The Revd. Dr. D. Stuart Dunnan
The Headmaster, Saint James School
Saint Albans, Class of 1977

A SERMON
AT THE EUCHARIST ON ALUMNI WEEKEND

These all died in faith, not having received what was promised,
but having seen it and greeted it from afar, and having
acknowledged that they were strangers and exiles on the earth.
For people who speak thus make it clear that they are seeking a
homeland. If they had been thinking of that land from which
they had gone out, they would have had opportunity to return.
But as it is, they desire a better country, that is, a heavenly one.
Hebrews 11:13–16

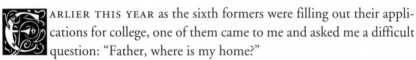ARLIER THIS YEAR as the sixth formers were filling out their applications for college, one of them came to me and asked me a difficult question: "Father, where is my home?"

Now you might think that the answer is a simple one: "Where do your parents live? What is the street address?" But in his case, the answer was not so simple, for his parents live in Saudi Arabia. They live in Saudi Arabia, but they are not Saudis; they are Pakistanis; they are also American citizens. This senior in fact was born in New York state and only moved to Saudi Arabia with his parents when he was in the fifth grade. In the tenth grade, he came to Saint James where he has boarded for three years; he is now the senior prefect. Now, I ask you, where is his home?

Another sixth former went for a walk with me some three years ago when he was a fourth former. He had just returned to school after his first summer vacation. He had spent his summer with his mother and stepfather in Johnstown and had visited his father in Cumberland. "It feels good to be home," he said, meaning good to be back at school.

A fifth former came to see me recently one evening after study hall to talk about the end of the year, his sixth-form friends who were graduating, and his fellow fifth formers scattering for the summer vacation. He was feeling, I think, prematurely "homesick," "homesick" for school, missing his friends already.

We were talking about graduation at dinner, and one sixth former who has boarded here for four years was speaking of two friends who have boarded here for the same four years with him. When I asked him who would cry the most, he insisted they would. One of his friends came over to join us; she agreed. Of course, she was going to cry; she was leaving "home."

As you know, I have only been here for five years, but now I have my own alumni: young men and women whom I have known and taught and lived with on this hill. And one of the great pleasures of having been here for five years is that they visit. I receive their letters and their phone calls, and now, of course, their e-mail. I am here when they stop by; they know where to find me; I get to hear their news. A recent graduate just stopped by the other day on his way back from college, and we had a good visit. It was good to see him as he stopped "home" on his way home.

And all the alumni and alumnae who have come back this weekend, many this year particularly to honor Father Owens and to celebrate their time here with him, haven't they all come "home?" Some faithfully every year, some more sporadically, some for the first time in many years, but all of them back "home."

The answer to my student's question is that "home" is many places: it is behind us, it is with us, it is ahead of us.

"Home" is not then that place in the past which our parents once built for us, frozen in time and lost to us for ever. "Home" rather begins with our parents and grows from the "home" they built for us to the "homes" we build ourselves. Their love for us is like a rock thrown into the water of life, creating for us that first expanding circle of love called "home." And this first circle of "home" grows into a second circle, a circle we build with new friendships and new relationships established by our own love for others. In this way, our parents' love for us, which creates that first "home" for us, grows in us and grows forth from us, creating even larger circles of "home" as we grow toward others in our lives.

And thus, our mothers' love for us which we honor and celebrate on this day, is meant to be a liberating and empowering love which goes out with us into the world. And even though a mother's first desire is to protect her child from challenge in the world, the good mother knows when to let go, in order to allow her child to grow beyond what she can establish or create towards what the child can establish and create: no longer her "home," but her child's "home."

And this is hard, for this requires sacrifice on the mother's part, a sacrifice which I see every time a mother decides to let her child board, to leave home and begin to create a new home. It is a generous action on her part, a venture of faith in her child and her child's ability to begin to build a new home beyond the one they share.

I remember when a fifth former moved into the dorm some two years ago. His mother told me that if I saw a flash of light up on the hill behind the school, it would be the sun reflected in the lens of her telescope. "Don't worry," I said, "you'll see him; you live close enough to do his laundry."

Consider the model of Our Lord's mother who supported Him in His ministry and watched Him in his suffering even on the cross: she gave Him His life and she allowed Him to offer His life in love and faith to others.

And this, of course, is the argument of the writer of the epistle to the Hebrews: we need to grow in this way. We are all of us called by our faith to grow in love and create "new homes" in the world, because we are all of us, like Abraham and Sarah, on a journey in our lives, journeying to "a land of promise," living "as in a foreign land," finding our homes "in tents." Like them, we are "strangers and exiles on the earth," but our faith in that promised "home" which lies ahead of us inspires us to journey and to build in love toward "a better country, that is, a heavenly one."

Thus, we cannot understand the purpose of our journey, or find the meaning of our lives if we cling fearfully to a "home" defined by our nuclear families. "Home" must be dynamic and expansive: growing ever larger, growing to include our neighbor and the stranger who can become our neighbor, even our friend.

And isn't this really, in the end, what Saint James is supposed to be about? Home and love; not in the static and the nuclear sense that our culture would use it, but in the broad and dynamic sense that Our Lord would use it? Haven't we found here the opportunity to love each other as teacher and student and friend and friend, really and substantially beyond the circle of our immediate families? Isn't this what the Saint James experience can bring to our students often for the first time?

For isn't this the first time that the circle of "home" can grow for our students outward from those to whom they are related by blood to include others to whom they are bound by a common experience which is constant and close? For in this place, a girl from Frederick and a boy from Washington, a boy from Thailand and a boy from Nigeria, a girl from West Virginia and a girl from Georgia can feel, by love, "related?"

Isn't this why students feel that they are coming "home" from "home" at the end of break, or alumni visit "home" on their way "home" from college, or come "home" again now several "homes" hereafter?

Didn't they discover that "home" expands here? That "home" is not just one place, but rather, many places? And not just a place defined by their family, but their friends, and not just their friends, but their new friends, even friends to come?

And didn't they discover that "home" can grow here and deepen here the more they reach out in love to others? The more they venture of themselves? Commit themselves? and offer themselves in friendship?

Who cares what color you are? Who cares what your parents do? Who cares whether you are a "star" in this or that endeavor? All that matters is whether you are committed to this community, and will build your "home" with us.

Because it is only by building in this way that Saint James can become for you the second of many "homes" in your life, a foundation for that larger "home," that next expanding circle, that "tent" upon your journey, that shelter for you to share with friends along your way, the earthly and temporary promise of that "heavenly [and permanent] country" which calls us all and unites us with the saints who have built this "home" before us.

Amen.

A Letter to Parents
Concerning Disciplinary Matters

Dear [   ]:

I write to inform you that your [son or daughter] was at a graduation party at which several recent Saint James alumni and some enrolled students drank beer and/or smoked marijuana.

As is usual when these parties happen, I have had several conversations with students who attended or who were sincerely concerned for their friends who did. As you know, I am an adult with some authority in their lives, and they rightly turn to me on those occasions when they are disappointed in each other or in themselves. I am proud of them in this regard: proud of their concern for each other, their concern for the reputation of the school, and their concern for our own relationships within the school as parents, teachers, and students.

Frankly, events such as these are divisive: they divide friends from each other, parents from their children, and indeed some parents from each other and from me as headmaster. I regret this obviously, just as I regret an occasion which afforded some of our students an opportunity to break the law and indulge in behaviors I do not tolerate on campus.

Though I recognize that the students who attended this party were on vacation and off campus and therefore their parents' responsibility, I am writing to you as their parents to ask you please to take this occasion to speak with your child about [his or her] behavior at this gathering. Some students responded quite well, and we should use this as an opportunity to affirm their good decisions; some did not, and we should use this as an opportunity to help them to learn from their mistakes, so they can make better decisions in the future.

In any case, I know about it; and this means that you should know about it. All of us make mistakes in raising young people: sometimes we trust them too much, sometimes we trust them too little. I have made both, and I am sure you have as well; it goes with the territory. Recognizing this and recognizing the ability of our students to make their own mistakes, I think it especially important that we speak honestly with each other about our concerns as we seek to raise them as best we can together.

A particular concern of mine is the distinction some students appear to draw between acceptable behavior "on campus" and "off campus." I know that some parents support them in this, and I would ask them not to. Let me just say honestly that students who smoke marijuana off campus or drink alcohol off campus tend to adopt attitudes and fall into patterns of behavior which bring these activities onto campus. They talk about it on campus in a way which makes students who do not engage in these activities feel uncomfortable and less than "popular;" they engage in these activities on campus and risk dismissal; and they disengage from more wholesome activities on campus in order to be off campus as much as possible.

Further, as I have stated before, I am concerned about the message that "what Father Dunnan doesn't know, won't hurt him." Let me just tell you that parents who cast me as the "heavy" in order to appear more "accepting" to their child tend to experience me as the "heavy" when their child proceeds to test me in my "limited" role as headmaster. To be blunt, they cut me off as a proactive resource to their family in addressing problems as they develop and set me up as a reactive disciplinarian when they lose control.

Obviously, the school reserves the right to protect its good name in these matters (Student Handbook, p. 9); but those of you who know me well, know that I do not respond in a disciplinary manner when I can avoid it. My concern in this matter is pastoral: I am concerned that our students who made good decisions be affirmed for these, that our students who made bad decisions learn from these, and that our parents understand that our students' behavior off campus necessarily affects their experience on campus, especially the integrity of their relationships with each other, with their teachers, and with me.

Yours faithfully,

The Revd. Dr. D. Stuart Dunnan
The Headmaster, Saint James School

AN ADDRESS
ON THE OCCASION OF THE INSTITUTION OF
ROBERT GRAVES AS HEAD OF HOLLAND
. HALL, TULSA, OKLAHOMA

*"For this commandment which I command you this day is not
too hard for you, neither is it far off. It is not in heaven, that you
should say, 'Who will go up for us to heaven, and bring it to us,
that we may hear it and do it?' But the word is very near you; it
is in your mouth and in your heart, so that you can do it."*
Deuteronomy 30:11–14

HEN BOB GRAVES ASKED ME TO SPEAK at his institution as the new Head of Holland Hall, I was, of course, flattered, and also pleased to say yes.

Mr. Graves and I have been friends since we started teaching history together at what was then Harvard School in Los Angeles back in 1981; we also worked together at Harvard School when he was Dean of Students and I was Assistant Chaplain.

In fact, I was with Mr. Graves at Harvard when he made the decision to come to Holland Hall. So when I met Diana Beebe and Paula Carreiro at the New Heads Conference some five years ago, I recognized the school from whence they came.

Through these friendships and through my own participation in the National Association of Episcopal Schools, I came to know Peter Branch as well, so I now often find myself in very enjoyable social situations where I am the only head of school present who has not worked here at Holland Hall.

Therefore, it is a special pleasure for me to be here with Mr. Graves and Mrs. Beebe on this important occasion, and also a pleasure to be here at

Holland Hall to see for myself this wonderful school I have heard so much about and to make this happy connection of friends to place.

Now, let me just say at the outset and for the record that I think you have chosen very well. I know that Mr. Graves loves this school very much, and I know that his commitment to you is sincere and absolute. Certainly, he enjoys many of the attributes we would look for in an effective head of school: a robust ego, an open heart, a critical mind, and a ready smile. Most importantly, he has a great sense of humor which has been the bedrock of our own close friendship, and which will prove I think his greatest resource through the years ahead.

Certainly, he has a wonderful wife; and I know that we can rely upon Julie Graves to keep her husband humble and penitent when appropriate, to compliment his own rather strong personality with her own equally strong personality, and to help him with his mistakes. Because, believe me, mistakes will come; they are part of the job.

When Mr. Graves called recently pretending to be excited that I was coming, but really making sure that I would not embarrass him publicly on such an important occasion, I asked him what my text would be. "I don't know," he said, "I guess whatever you want."

Now, let me just say by way of apology that this is not a very Episcopalian approach to the liturgy. As I am sure most of you know, Episcopal priests are used to an assigned text appropriate to the day in the liturgical year. But your headmaster has yet to be canonized, so there is no Saint Robert Graves Day that I can turn to in the calendar of lesser feasts and fasts. At least, not yet . . .

But as I thought about what I would like to say to you on this occasion and what passage of Scripture might be appropriate, it occurred to me that there is a particular figure in the Bible who does speak to me of my own experience as the head of an Episcopal school.

Interestingly, (at least to me) this is not the figure I would have chosen when I began as headmaster some five years ago. I think if you had asked me about my role then, I would have looked to Our Lord's image of the Good Shepherd; I would have seen myself and of course in many ways still see myself as the tender and careful shepherd of my flock.

But the actual work of shepherding my flock, the job of protecting them and leading them in today's world, has made me consider the story of Moses in a new and more compelling light. I find myself much more sympathetic to him than I used to be and much more appreciative of the challenges and opportunities which he faced as the leader of God's people on their journey out of Egypt towards the promised land.

And I think if you will consider the story of Moses with me, you will see how he presents to us a model and an icon for faithful leadership which speaks particularly to the head of an Episcopal school. Allow me to list some parallels:

First, as a leader, Moses served a greater mission: God's mission, God's plan to free His chosen people from their bondage in Egypt and to bring them to the promised land. If you recall, this was not particularly Moses's mission until God called him through that burning bush. Certainly, Moses bravely denied his Egyptian upbringing and got himself exiled by assuming the cause of his fellow Hebrews, but this is only a first step which led to other steps in a journey he never would have imagined, and certainly not assumed if he had known what in fact awaited him.

And so it is with the head of school. Someone asked me after my first year or so if I ever actually realized what my job would be like. I had no idea, and I have yet to meet any head of school who did. Mr. Graves may be an exception because he has had a year as your interim head, but I expect that he will be as surprised as all the rest of us; and not just surprised once, but surprised often: indeed, every month, every week, every day.

Get ready, Mr. Graves, because I am here to tell you that you begin, this day, a journey, and you have no idea where this journey will take you. You are not in control of it; it is bigger than you. And the voice which calls you and directs you on this journey will speak to you from many burning bushes and on many mountains, in many conversations and crises and really quite ordinary moments along the way. Just remember to take off your shoes, because you will walk on holy ground.

Secondly, as a human being, Moses was profoundly aware of his own inadequacy, his own need as a human being for help in his new role as leader of the people of God. And God gave him help: he gave him that wonderful staff to terrify Pharaoh, and He commissioned Moses's brother Aaron to speak for him. Later, during the Exodus, God encouraged Moses to appoint priests and judges under him to be many places for Moses, because Moses had finally learnt that he could be only one place at a time.

Here again, the good head of school knows that he or she is inadequate. It takes a while for us to figure it out, and certainly takes a very long while for the rest of our communities to figure it out; but only God is God, and Mr. Graves cannot do it all.

As much as he will want to be and as much as many will expect him to be, he cannot be on the phone, writing a letter, giving a speech, counselling a student, presiding at several meetings, and attending six different sports and cultural events all at the same time. He will get pretty good at faking it, but he will never actually be able to do it. There is after all, only one Holy Spirit.

So this means that he will need help from able and faithful administrators and teachers, supportive and committed trustees, parents, alumni, and student leaders. God will call you as well, and you will need to work together, to help and support each other in your common life and purpose at this school.

Thirdly, Moses served as the link between his people and the outside world, speaking for them to Pharaoh: presenting their cause, making their argument, serving their best interest.

In the same way, the head of school is the one who speaks for the school to the outside world and engages in that whole inside/outside conversation which connects our schools as communities with the wider communities we serve.

And the good head does not just speak to the outside world, but also like Moses listens to the outside world, engages in the argument, hearing the concerns and the needs that are "out there" and bringing them "in here" that they may be addressed within the fold.

And this role on the part of the head is essential to the health and future of a school. Independent schools, especially when they are strong, are sometimes tempted to attend only to voices internal and to engage only in conversations within: to do what they do well and to refuse to consider those voices on the outside which would criticize and challenge their assumptions and practices. We cannot afford this.

But neither can we afford to ignore the ignorance and willfulness of Pharaoh and let our people linger with his bricks. We need to speak to the pharaohs of our time and defend our schools, pursuing the good purposes, and proclaiming the enduring values for which we stand. More people need to understand us: why we do what we do, and why what we do works. The mission we serve is the right one.

Fourthly, Moses served as the link between his community as it existed and the goal which challenged it into the future; in short, the link between his community and God. He journeyed up that mountain to find the truth and discern the way ahead; and he returned with that truth and led in that way, because he himself believed in it. When he spoke with his people, he spoke to challenge them, even as he loved them.

In the same way, the head of school lives in that tension between what is now and what can be, always challenging and always reminding the community of the school to serve the vision which inspires it. The great imperative to love which comes from God is moral, not sentimental; and the head who answers to God for the direction of the school must be absolutely committed to walk in this moral way of love ahead.

Certainly, the greatest change which I have experienced in my short life so far was the change in my role from being a college chaplain to being a headmaster: I went from being everybody's friend to being everybody's boss. The cause of love remained the same, but the role was a new one. As the leader of the school, the head must be willing to climb that mountain alone and to engage in those mountain conversations which will make his time below both more lonely and more difficult.

In this regard, I often remember the advice of Father Owens, who served as headmaster of Saint James for twenty-nine years before me. He told me when I became headmaster: "do not worry whether it is popular or not, just worry whether it is right or wrong." In short, listen to your mountain conversations; don't just play to the crowd.

And so, finally, Moses led his community on a journey, seeking a new, promised land which they had never seen. He did not settle with them into a nice comfortable existence; rather he encouraged them to move on, to embrace the greater challenges ahead in faith and love together. This will be Mr. Graves's job, and this will be your job, as you make this journey as a community together.

But remember that the greatest temptation along the way which can distract you from the way remains the same temptation which often distracted the Hebrews: it remains idolatry.

And let us be honest: schools are full of golden calves. There will always be parents who think that this community exists for parents, students who think that it exists for students, faculty for faculty, alumni for alumni, donors for donors. They are all of them wrong: this community exists for God.

And beware achievement for achievement's sake; this is a subtler form of idolatry which can easily infect our schools. Achieve for the journey: which is to say, achieve for the vision, achieve for that great cause of Love which inspires and sustains us all.

Like any community of faith founded for a faithful purpose, indeed like that first community of the Hebrews, this community of Holland Hall, this the Episcopal school in Tulsa, Oklahoma, must live for the Love of God and shine with the Love of God in a world otherwise distracted and usually unimpressed. This is why you teach in this place: you teach to transform the world. Make sure you teach the right lessons for the right reasons for the right purposes.

And as this community journeys as a school towards the future in faith together, so each individual in this community—teacher, parent, and student—should journey forth from this place inspired and empowered with that vision of self-giving Love revealed to us in the teaching of the prophets and in the life and witness of Jesus Christ Our Lord. For this is the vision which should distinguish you as an Episcopal school and this is the vision which should call you forward into your future. With this vision, you will shine; and by this vision, you will serve the world.

So now, at this moment on your journey, you have chosen this good man Bob Graves to lead you, and this is what we celebrate. Know that he is human and that the mission he serves is greater than all of us, much too great for him alone to accomplish. Therefore, support him, help him, and join with him on this great journey; make it your own: yours and his together.

Amen.

A Sermon
Thoughts on the Battle of Antietam
and the Enduring Legacy
of John Barrett Kerfoot,
Parent's Weekend

Jesus said, "Every one then who hears these words of mine and
does them will be like a wise man who built his house upon the
rock; and the rain fell, and the floods came, and the winds
blew and beat upon that house, but it did not fall, because it
had been founded on the rock."
Matthew 7:24–25

THIS YEAR, THE SECOND WEEKEND IN SEPTEMBER, some 12,000 reenactors staged a very effective reenactment of the Battle of Antietam at the Artz Farm just off Rench Road which is down the railroad tracks from school; and I have to admit that the scale of the reenactment and its quality continued to impress me as it developed over the weekend.

It really was quite remarkable to be awakened by the sound of artillery fire early in the morning as we were that Saturday, and quite sobering to think what it must have been like to have been at Saint James when the real Battle of Antietam opened with such terrible force just down the Sharpsburg Pike 135 years ago. Hearing the artillery fire, I remembered an excerpt from Dr. Kerfoot's diary:

Wednesday, September 17—Awakened early, 5 to 6, by fearful cannonading
from battlefield (as yesterday, but worse). We watched anxiously from top of the
College. At one time musketry, fearful and prolonged for an hour. Artillery

more than a hundred peals a minute. both armies seemed to hold ground. The noise lessened near noon. Fearful, anxious morning! [1]

When I read this passage in chapel on Monday morning after the reenactment, the boarders had knowing looks on their faces: "five to six" was just when we were awakened, too.

The Revd. Dr. John Barrett Kerfoot was our first rector, and he built Saint James from our foundation as a school and college in 1842. At the time of the Civil War, Saint James was entirely Kerfoot's creation, considered by sources as distinguished as General Robert E. Lee and President Sparks of Harvard to be one of the finest institutions in the south. That he should have built a school with such a strong academic reputation from nothing in a matter of a few years is really a remarkable achievement.

Certainly, I have found that any time that I make any kind of foray into the history of the school, there stands Kerfoot at our founding, larger than life, by all contemporary accounts a hero in his generation, a great builder priest and a bold educator of strongly held principles, a man of remarkable faith and vision, as brave as he was dedicated.

When some students were working in the archives this summer, they came across Kerfoot's speech at the dedication of Kemp Hall, a building which still stands as a monument to him despite the ravages of fire and of time. The speech was in his own hand, and the years seemed to melt away as we looked at his text. Today, Kemp Hall remains at the heart of our school, restored and rebuilt by us again as a center for our students, our alumni, and our faculty.

Obviously, as headmaster, I often think of Kerfoot and how he must have felt facing the considerable challenges of his time. Proud as I am of the school and all that we have accomplished these last few years, and proud as I am of our students and of our faculty, I can, I think, appreciate how he felt, his own sense of accomplishment and fulfillment, as he worked to improve and strengthen this community of Saint James.

But then, he was the founder; and I, like all between us, am only one who follows him. He had to build this place from scratch and then fight hard to preserve it in the midst of the Civil War; so I would have to feel very sorry for myself, indeed, if I were ever to consider the small challenges which I have faced to be anything approaching his.

---

[1] H. Harrison, *Life of Kerfoot* (New York, 1886) vol. i, p. 235.

And he, of course, was forced to face the ultimate challenge: he had to give it up; all that he had built and all that he had worked for, some 22 years of his life; he had to abandon it as lost in August of 1864, lost to the ravages of war around him.

Happily, Kerfoot's words at his last public commencement in 1862 would prove prophetic:

> *It is our hope and resolve to keep our College alive, and busy in so much of this work as God may now send it; and ready for full work when he shall restore to us the usual scope and demand for it. Today we choose not to measure our college by the mere present. We think of the 712 pupils who, through 20 years have been under our tuition. And we remember, too how often the hours and the youth that seemed to promise no fruit in requital for our efforts, have turned out before our own eyes the most fruitful hours and hearts in our record. So do we care the less today that the times have left us but three graduates, when we know that these make up the fair, satisfying sum of 91 graduates at 15 commencements. We expect to send out many more good men such as we now know among the hundreds who have been here. But, even if this were not our hope now, none of us would deem the past a vain expenditure of time and work for any of us.*[2]

Still, what remains for us to celebrate about Kerfoot is not just his confidence in Saint James, its campus or its buildings, or even the achievement of its students or its academic standing under his care. Certainly, he worked hard to achieve these good things; but none of them to him were ends in themselves. They were, rather, always means to a greater end, the purpose of love he believed in and served so faithfully in his life. Indeed, if Kerfoot took pride in anything, it was in the quality of the society of Saint James, the way Saint James functioned as a community even then, the spirit of love and good fellowship which inspired it and gave evidence to the greater cause he believed in. Thus, he continues in his speech:

> *It is not in pride or boast that we thus speak: it is in gratitude to God; it is to justify Him from our own experience of his mercies here; it is to encourage and reassure our own hearts and the hearts of all who care for us and our work. How the college and its government will bear itself amid the strifes of the times, the de-*

---

[2] Harrison, i, pp. 230–231.

*clarations made here a year ago, and the independent, prudent, impartial ac-
complishment since, sufficiently show that here, in harmony, on an equality,
and amid some fair measure of efficient working, young men may yet meet and
live together, to learn how personal affections and courtesy ought to and may
smooth down the ill-tempers and distrusts that ought never to have arisen. Is not
this, the one last collegiate home of such peace in the latitude, worth the effort to
perpetuate it? Is it not worth the mutual forbearance and self-denial required of
you, my young friends? May it not be your best discipline for such tasks of peace
and harmony in State and Church as your God may have in early store for some
of you? We think of all this, and so we work on yet, and until God bids us stop.
We hear no such bidding yet. And should that word come to us, none the less has
the work thus far done been worth the while. It will stand. It will repeat itself
through other agencies in better times.[3]*

And now that we find ourselves in better times when the artillery which
awakens us is for fun and not for real, the number of the reenactors themselves only approaching the number of the dead at the battle they would reen-
act, men in grey and men in blue, laughing and joking in a mixed company
of friends as they walk together to the parking lot, feeling still the heat and the
dust of a late summer's afternoon; now that we find ourselves in just that time
of peace which Dr. Kerfoot prayed for, is it not remarkable that the vision
which inspires us remains the same as his? And is it not also remarkable that
this vision requires Saint James to be different in our time even as it required
Saint James to be different in his?

When Dr. Kerfoot looked to Saint James and commended it to the young
of 1862, he pointed to that spirit of love which distinguished it as a society and
made it a model he hoped for America at large. So now we also look to Saint
James for the same witness and the same ministry, build and preserve it still as
a place apart, guided in faith by Our Lord's enduring imperative to love. And
we commend it as he did, now to young women as well as men, to students
from several countries, not just our own, to the young of 1997, threatened not
so much by the fear of war as by the complacency which comes with peace, by
the ravages of privation as by the blandishments of prosperity, the siren song
of selfishness which surrounds us. Our song, our appeal is a different one:
come here and be otherwise; be otherwise for good as we in faith receive it;

---

[3] Harrison, i, p. 231.

learn here how to love and serve your neighbor faithfully; and seek here that kingdom of God which endures.

John Barrett Kerfoot built Saint James; we are only preserving it, and building again on his sure foundation; and not merely the foundation of land and brick we see around us, or even the foundation of those solid accomplishments achieved by those who have served Saint James as he did before us, rather the invisible and the intangible foundation of his faith and his courage, his willingness, indeed his eagerness for us to be different, to stand apart in little things and in great things, in the challenges of war and the challenges of peace, to live differently as a society; in his words, "to learn how personal affections and courtesy ought to and may smooth down the ill tempers and distrusts that ought never to have arisen."

This is the rock on which Saint James was founded, and this is the rock on which we stand.

Amen.

An Essay
Girls at Saint James

I WAS HOSTING VISITORS RECENTLY, introducing them to students and to faculty, showing them our buildings, several of course recently renovated and constructed, and they were impressed by so much evidence of improvement and progress. Turning to me, one of them asked me what I thought was the most significant change in the school since I became headmaster. I considered some choices: the new arts center, the new library, the improvement in college placement, a new first form and expanded middle school; the list was a long one. But then as I thought about it, the choice was obvious: girls.

As I think back over the last six years since I came to Saint James, the population of girls and the program for girls have grown and developed at a natural, reasonable pace which belies the great significance of their impact. Further, because the girls' program has progressed within a wider context of improvement and progress, we have not always focused on the girls as the success story that they are. In a way, this has been good in that the girls' program has been driven "from below" more than "from above:" it is largely the girls themselves who have established it. Thus, the particular steps in this growth have been, in the right sense, inevitable.

Let us review the recent history. In September of 1976, Jenny Mott, Molly Moody, and Lori Grimm came as the first three "pioneers." Sisters and neighbors, they came as day students, and they came to stay. Gradually, their number grew, and girls were admitted in every subsequent year. The next step was girls' boarding which began the year before I arrived: 1991. In that year, there were thirteen girls boarding on the top floor of Hershey Hall. That summer, we added the ground floor, and the number of girls boarding grew to nineteen; there are now twenty-two with a waiting list. Hence, the need for a new girls' dorm. The total number of girls when I arrived was thirty; this year there are sixty-six.

Obviously, this growth in our contingent of girls has led to some changes, most notably in athletics. Katharine Byron '84 remembers the days when girls' athletics was stuffing admissions envelopes; I remember when we only offered one sport in each season: field hockey, aerobics, and tennis. In my time, we have added three competitive sports to the girls' program: first, basketball in the winter, then lacrosse in the spring, and most recently, soccer in the fall. In addition, girls continue to participate with the boys in cross country, golf, and squash.

I still remember when I asked Mr. Barr and Mr. Hoyer to coach the first girls' basketball team; it was the very definition of a "building year." I was thinking back to those days and the bewildered and anguished looks on Mr. Hoyer's face during those games, as I watched our present girls' basketball team compete brilliantly in this year's very successful season. I also remember starting up the girls' lacrosse team again (I understand Mrs. Baker coached an earlier team when Father Baker was headmaster). Mr. Meehan was excited to hire a very effective coach who was then an undergraduate at Shippensburg. "Coach K" as she was then is now "Miss Koretke," a full-time member of our faculty teaching math, dorm parenting in Hershey, and yes, still coaching.

Our key coaches when I arrived here were all school mothers: in field hockey, Carol Van Reenan, mother of Chip '83 and Dennis '87, and Bonnie Parks, mother of Andy '90; in tennis, Chris Randall, mother of Laura '89, Leigh '89, and Lesley '95. These coaches were also pioneers. They established strong, competitive programs in their respective sports which have continued after them, and they were passionate advocates for girls' athletics and for the girls' place at Saint James generally.

Annabel Wait '81 (now Griffin) once asked me if the Headmaster's Prize was still given to "a scholar and a gentleman." When I explained that we had updated the wording to "a lady or gentleman," she was disappointed. She confessed that it gave her a certain pleasure to walk past all those "gentlemen" as she walked to the steps to receive it. In my time, I have watched many young women take that walk to receive academic and school prizes at commencement. I have not made a scientific study of it, but I suspect that the number of prizes won by girls at Saint James is disproportionate to the percentage of girls in each class, highlighting, I think, the particular character of a Saint James woman: graceful and gracious certainly, but also strong, talented, and ambitious, ready to achieve and more than willing to beat the boys in the classroom.

Setting aside the social benefit of girls which is a topic requiring several essays itself, the extracurricular benefit has been enormous. The Chapel Choir now boasts strong soprano and alto sections, and it is difficult to imagine the Mummers without the consistent contribution of a steady succession of leading ladies on the stage. Interestingly, student publications have benefited as well, particularly the *Bai Yuka* which has usually been headed by a girl senior editor ever since I have been here. Girls have also helped to raise the visual arts to a much higher standard during these past six years; I think particularly of Beth Powell '93 and Eva Wylie '97.

I think the girls' dorm has a great deal to do with the confidence of our girls because of the strong feeling of "us girls" which the dorm encourages. Girls' athletics has also helped: the proven ability of our girls to pull a team together and to compete against larger teams from larger schools with remarkable, even miraculous success. Ironically, being a minority within the student body has helped, encouraging the girls to support each other as young women and to compete with the boys more confidently. Finally, I think that Saint James is the key: our character as a small school which treats our students as individuals and our moral commitment as a Church school to mutual respect and equality between men and women; we see this now in the visible leadership of strong and talented women on campus, most notably Sandra Pollock, the Academic Dean.

But again, the progression has been a natural one, it has not been contrived: during my time, three women faculty have grown to twelve, two girl prefects have grown to three, next year, four. The senior sacristan this year is a girl, not because she is a girl, but because she is Sarah Delashmutt who was the obvious choice. I guess, in the end, this is my point: what has been won and achieved here, has been won and achieved by the girls themselves, and they have benefited as individuals from their participation in this achievement as much as we have benefited as a school from their leadership and contribution. This has been what has been the most fun and the most inspiring for me to watch: the individual successes within the greater achievement. I look at the whole phenomenon with some pride, but I remember the girls themselves with more.

And let me just make this point. The boys in the end have benefited as much as the girls, in that they have had the opportunity to learn with young women and thus to respect and work with them properly. As we know all too well from recent sad stories in the media, men who hope to succeed in today's America need to know how to function appropriately in a mixed workplace;

we need to know how to respect and work with women as colleagues and superiors. Young men growing up at Saint James are learning how to do this during a time in their lives and in a popular culture which can often tempt them to objectify young women, rather than respect them. I am therefore particularly proud of the fact that boys and girls can be friends at Saint James, fellow students, fellow Jacobites, that they can live and work together in a shared community which feels in their own words "like a family."

Therefore, as we anticipate the final stage of the Quadrangle Campaign and watch with gratitude the construction of the new girls' dormitory, we do well, I think, to look back over these past twenty-two years with some pride. And we do well to remember that it is the girls of Saint James who have built Saint James as the wonderful place for girls and for boys that we are becoming. Their achievement is remarkable and remains in our present and for our future their own, enduring gift.

Spring 1998

A Sermon
Alumni Weekend

Do not be deceived, my beloved brethren. Every good
endowment and every perfect gift is from above, coming down
from the Father of lights with whom there is no variation or
shadow due to change.

James 1:16–17

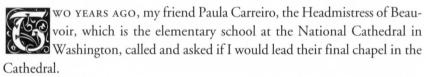WO YEARS AGO, my friend Paula Carreiro, the Headmistress of Beau-
voir, which is the elementary school at the National Cathedral in
Washington, called and asked if I would lead their final chapel in the
Cathedral.

Flattered to the core, I assumed that she was asking me because I was an
alumnus and my niece was in the second grade, or because my liturgical fame
had spread from Hagerstown back to Washington, or even just because we
were friends. She quickly dispelled my presumptions: the dean of the Cathedral who normally led the service had jury duty, so they were stranded. She
knew she could count on me to say yes.

And, of course, I said yes; and I appeared on time some two days later at
9:30 for the 10:00 service. Upon my arrival, I was immediately ushered to the
office of the teacher coordinating the liturgy and offered a seat in her office.

"What are you going to say in your address?" she asked.

"What address?" I asked in return.

"Your address," she insisted.

"What do you mean?" I pleaded.

Her eyes filled with a kind look of pity and compassion. "Didn't you know
that this is our graduation, and that you are the graduation speaker?"

94

At this stage, I had 15 minutes to walk over to the Cathedral, get vested, and write my speech in my mind. I decided to get over there as quickly as I could.

As I walked to the Cathedral, talking to myself like a lunatic, I considered the challenge before me as rationally as I could and began to calm down. After all, I assured myself, I was speaking to a group of elementary school children, and they would not be expecting anything profound. I could "go with the flow," and "wing it" when the time came to say something. I even began to wonder what I might want to say; things were looking up.

And then I entered the Cathedral. It was full: both transepts and the nave appeared completely full. The place was full of parents; and what made these parents particularly terrifying was that some of them were childhood friends of mine who had also grown up on the Cathedral Close. Several rushed up full of pride in their children, eager to greet me: "We were so pleased to hear that you were speaking." The hidden message was obvious: "Don't mess up."

"Speaking:" there was that word again; what in the world was I to say to them. I went to the slype and vested, deep in fervent and anxious prayer, and then processed to the crossing, deeper into the nightmare of it all.

The third graders took their places on the steps behind me, and the rest of the school sat cross-legged on the Cathedral floor in a full circle around me. Mothers and fathers darted about madly, taking photographs. As I looked at all those adorable upturned faces, aglow with the excitement of this very important moment in their young and fragile lives, I felt more fragile myself, a bit like Charles I on trial before Cromwell's Parliament. What in the world was I going to say to them?

Everyone sang the Beauvoir song: very cute, but also very short. The third graders did a Maypole dance: also very cute, and fortunately a bit longer. I found myself wondering if pagan rituals belonged in sacred spaces. And then, my turn; Mrs. Carreiro introduced me to the children: "Father Dunnan is the headmaster of a boarding school. How many of you have ever heard of a boarding school? . . ." The words blurred in my mind; the nightmare was getting worse.

And then it came to me. I would talk to them about what I had been talking to Saint James about; what I always talk to Saint James about this time of year: saying goodbye, and saying thank you.

Stalling for time, I asked the third graders how they thought they should say goodbye; and then, after one of them gave me the answer I wanted, I continued to develop my theme: "to whom should you say thank you?"

"My teachers," offered one little boy; "my friends," said another, "my best friend," said a little girl; "my parents," said another; we were "on a roll." Then, one very clever child who obviously has a career in government service offered "Mrs. Carreiro" to a warm reception of general approval and appreciation.

The feeling was perfect, the atmosphere could not have been friendlier. Students and teachers and parents were all of them deservedly very proud; fathers were jingling their change and mothers were reaching for their handkerchiefs; many throats were cleared in the emotion of the moment.

And then, I asked my final question: "Anyone else?" Blank looks. "Is there any one else you should thank?" A sea of blank looks.

Then one of the students offered a strange, unthought of answer tentatively as a question: "God?" she asked.

The looks all around were embarrassed: "Whoops, we forgot." In that great and beautiful cathedral dedicated to the glory of God, God is the answer who was not on the tips of their tongues.

This weekend, we have celebrated a great deal, and we have said many well deserved thank you's, for we are surrounded by grace; indeed, "grace upon grace," thank you's for thank you's for thank you's.

Generous Alumni and parents grateful for all that they learned and experienced in this place have built buildings to say thank you in needed and valuable ways: thank you to Father Owens, most especially, but also thank you to generations of teachers and friends who touched and changed their lives for the better while they were here.

And we, those of us who live and work here now, we say thank you back: thank you for believing in us still and for helping us to be better in our continuing mission of learning and of love.

For indeed, this whole school lives on love, given and received and given back again, captured most powerfully in the faithful expression of gratitude. All around us on a weekend like this, we hear and see the thank you's offered, and we feel in our hearts the magic which is Saint James: the love of teachers and students, friends and friends which speaks to the very purpose of this remarkable school. We care about each other, and we care enough to say "thank you."

But let there never be silence when we ask ourselves that next, more vital question: "Whom else should we thank?"

Let us always thank God. For we need to thank God, and we need to thank God for two essential reasons:

First, we need to thank God, because without God none of this would be possible. He has brought us together, and not just with each other, but with all who have built this place before us, to share in their legacy. He has challenged us in every generation to preserve and improve, restore and renew the essence of Saint James, inspiring those who went before us to set the right example and encouraging us who follow to continue in their way.

He has given us this good land in which to build this school, our country with its freedoms, and our peace with its prosperity. He has revealed to us the very truths which we would teach here; and He has made us in His image, so that we can learn and teach these truths, even in our humanity. He has given us life; each of us, you and me life, that we may share our lives and build our lives together. And He has shown us in Christ the way of life which is love: His life which can be our life, if only we will join Him in His own enduring purpose. He provides, in short, what He has always provided: the grace to combine and to transform the meager sum of us into a valuable and great treasure.

Secondly, we need to thank God, because if we do not, this school becomes idolatrous. Saint James has become again a very strong school. Our campus is impressive, and our students are doing well. There are now more qualified candidates who wish to attend this place than we can accept. Like gods, we can choose, and like fools we can take false comfort in these signs of strength around us. We can say to ourselves, as so many other independent schools have made the mistake of saying before us: "We are perfect; we are wonderful; we are divine. Let us worship our faculty, and worship our students and worship these buildings, for we have made them."

But this would be false. Only God is divine; we are only human. To God belongs the glory, not to us; because the moment we steal the glory from God, we fail to be self-critical, and we fail to be faithful to the continuing challenge of discipleship.

Surely then, if we would honor Father Owens on this his weekend, this is the truth which we should take again to heart; because this is the truth which he believes in and kept so faithfully before this community when he was headmaster. Like all the good headmasters before him, he did not build a temple here with many graven images to be worshiped and adored, but a home for the young, a place for them to grow and to learn in fellowship with each other and their teachers the truths which are eternal.

"Every good endowment and every perfect gift is from above," even, no especially, Saint James School. We have the miracles, and we have the saints to prove it.

Blessed then be God our Heavenly Father who has given us this good gift to share and to fashion in His own enduring purpose.

Amen.

Fall 1998

An Essay
"Thank you for giving me back my daughter": the truth about boarding school in late twentieth century America.

Written for the Vincent/Curtis Education Register

INTRODUCTION

Two years ago, during Parents' Weekend in the fall, a mother of a new eleventh-grade boarding student came up to me at the field hockey match, and said, "Thank you for giving me back my daughter."

I was then beginning my fifth year as headmaster, and I had heard similar comments from other parents before, so I paid close attention to what she said and decided to count how many times I would hear such a comment that day. As I recall, I heard the comment three times: two from parents regarding their daughters; one from parents regarding their son. Interestingly, for a school which has day as well as boarding students, they were all parents of boarding students.

As the headmaster of a boarding school, I obviously believe in the boarding experience; and I would be a fraud if I did not. In my life at school, I experience every day the deeper relationships and greater opportunities for growth and learning which boarding provides. But I am also the head of a school in a part of the country where boarding schools like mine are somewhat rare and the boarding experience is viewed by parents, even day parents within my own school, with a great deal of emotional resistance and distrust.

D. Stuart Dunnan

Certainly, the decision to board your child is always a difficult one for any parent; it is emotionally "loaded." As I argued in my last article for this publication,[1] it requires on the part of parents a very generous act of love: a willingness to pay more, to trust more, and to share in the venture of parenting. As I have watched parents struggle with this decision during my time here, I have come to appreciate that there are many assertions made by parents who resist the decision to board their child which are in fact more mythical than true.

And here I admit again that my own perspective is subjective, determined as it is by my good experience as an educator at a boarding school, and my confirmed confidence in what boarding can do. Thus, I am not speaking from the perspective of a parent of a high school student at home; that perspective remains your own. What I propose to do in this essay is to challenge you from my perspective to consider the assertions which I most often hear to justify a decision against boarding. I challenge you to look to the reality of your child's experience of school and the reality of your neighborhood and family life as it impacts your child's nurture and education to see if boarding does not make more sense rationally than you are perhaps willing to concede emotionally.

In my experience, the usual assertions against boarding school are of two kinds: myths about school, and myths about home.

MYTHS ABOUT SCHOOL

1) *The local school is the best school.* Often, perhaps even usually, this assertion is true. The local public school or the local private school is often just the right school for your child, particularly if the area in which you live provides some choice. But different students have different needs, and the neighborhood school is not always the best place for your child to grow and to learn. Indeed, each child in a family is different, and just because the local school was perfect for one child does not mean that it will fall within the acceptable to perfect range for the next. Similarly, the local K-12 day school which was just right for your child in elementary school and middle school, may not be the place for your child in high school.

---

[1] D. Stuart Dunnan, "I would never send my child to a boarding school . . ," (Vincent/Curtis Education Register 1995–1996).

2) *If the local school is not the best school for my child, then it "has" to be the best school.* We all know the phenomenon of angry parents insisting that the local school completely reorder itself in order to serve the particular needs of their own child. They want their child to go to the prestigious school, but they complain that it is too challenging; they want their child to go to a safe school, but they object that it is too strict on drugs; they want a school with values, but they complain it is too religious. The list goes on.

Usually, what has happened is that a family has chosen a school as acceptable because it is local, but they only like part of the program or ethos of the place. Sometimes, they feel trapped by their location: this is the *only* school. Thus, they plan to enter the school like Greeks into Troy: they come in smiling, but they come to subvert. This phenomenon also happens to parents who enter a school community for one child who is well served by the place, give to it generously and assume positions of leadership within it, but then discover that it is not the right school for the next child. According to them, this is clearly the school's fault.

The problem with the angry parent, of course, is that they are like a warm drop of lemon juice in a cold glass of milk, and their child is drinking the curdled result. They destroy the "taste" of school for their child and for anyone else who will listen to them within the school community, and thus isolate their child from his or her teachers and the school's administration. School becomes a battleground, the head of school the enemy, and the faculty function on a sliding scale from martyred allies to Gestapo agents. Meanwhile, the clock of youth is ticking, and the opportunity to teach and raise their child in a more positive and helpful environment is being lost forever.

3) *Boarding schools are all for "problem" kids.* Some boarding schools are indeed for "problem" kids. Because they are residential and therefore self-determining, boarding schools have the opportunity to find their individual niche and thus to serve the students whom they choose to enroll. Some boarding schools are very good at serving students with particular learning differences, for instance, or students with particular behavioral issues, or indeed combinations of the two.

Sometimes parents who are having relationship issues with their children, caused by divorce or remarriage, difficult sibling relationships, or parental issues of closeness and control are well advised to choose boarding school to insert more distance or more independence safely into their relationships with their children. Now, all of these children may be perceived by the neighbors as "problems," but usually they are not; and often a good experience at the appropriate boarding school will prove it.

Nonetheless, most boarding schools are not for "problem" kids. They are in fact for good kids who want to live at school in order to engage more fully in the things that happen at school: the student who wants more time to work and to interact with faculty, the athlete who wants to be part of a stronger team in a stronger program, the artist who wants more substantial opportunities with other students of talent in the arts, the "great kid" who has the kind of personal gifts or personal needs to benefit from learning and living in community.

Again, boarding schools provide a choice, and each student should be choosing a boarding school for his or her own particular combination of reasons. But the journey to boarding school does not always begin with a "problem" in the family or even a "problem" in the neighborhood or the local school; it begins more usually with a "promise" in the student yet to be fulfilled.

4) *Boarding schools are only for "rich" kids.* Because most boarding schools are private and because they are expensive to run, most boarding schools charge a substantial sum in tuition, typically more than the comparable private day schools. Indeed, the tuition charged by many boarding schools, particularly in the mid-Atlantic region and in New England, sometimes approaches the amount charged by small liberal arts colleges.

Because most middle-class people did not expect to pay for school, let alone boarding school, these tuitions come as a shock, and they assume quite reasonably that only "rich" kids go to these schools. This is not true. Many boarding schools have substantial endowments and use these endowments to support a large number of their students with tuition assistance. In fact, the proportion of a student body on scholarship at a well-established boarding school is typically much larger than the proportion at the comparable private day school. Further, there are many boarding schools like my own which use their endowments to keep their tuitions down, actually costing only a little more than the comparable day school.

Therefore, do not be scared away by a boarding school's tuition. If your child is a good candidate and if you can demonstrate genuine financial need in meeting the cost of tuition, then most schools can and will help.

5) *Boarding schools are only for "WASPs."* This myth is perfectly understandable, but also now untrue. Almost all boarding schools, certainly the historic ones, were founded for the sons and daughters of the white, Anglo-Saxon, Protestant elite who governed this nation in the nineteenth century. Some

schools were founded with a more charitable purpose, and the Roman Catholics responded with schools of their own; but the whole phenomenon of boarding school was based upon the model of the great English public schools like Winchester and Eton. This model appealed to English, largely Episcopalian Americans because it appealed to their anglophilia and their desire to model the education of their children on the education of the governing classes in England.

Today, these schools still stand as perhaps the most famous boarding schools in America; but America has changed, and so have boarding schools generally. With the advent and growth of strong local private schools in most urban areas, the social and economic elite who used to send their children to boarding school no longer send them automatically. Strong interest in American education from abroad, the higher priority which some newer immigrant families place on education, and the ability of boarding schools to support a larger number of students on scholarship have all made the typical boarding school campus much more diverse than that of the typical private day school or even the good public high school in a wealthy suburban neighborhood.

Indeed, even the very "Englishness" of many of our schools has made them especially appealing to international students and recent professional immigrants from African and Asian countries formerly ruled by the British. To such families of color, our schools look more familiar than the local American public high school. School communities in which teachers are treated with respect and trusted with co-parental authority to join in the work of raising one's children, strike parents from more traditional cultures as stronger schools and more effective. Further, charitable foundations, churches, and families which support minority students of promise recognize that these students often need a boarding environment if they are going to learn how to interact successfully with a wider variety of people and succeed with a more demanding academic curriculum.

Boarding schools therefore are typically more diverse socioeconomically and racially than comparable private day schools, sometimes dramatically so. The result of this diversity can be magical, and it offers in microcosm a vision of our world to come. Sharing the strong community and the common experiences of the school where they live, young people come to feel related as "family" and easily transcend the differences of nationality, culture, race, religion, region and wealth. By living and studying together, they quickly discover and then constantly assume the common aspects of our humanity. This does not mean that differences are forgotten, because of course they are not; but it does mean that differences are questioned, challenged and honored in countless late-night conversations and anxious discussions inspired by honest curiosity and emboldened by genuine friendship. As one of my students commented recently, we function like the bridge of the Starship Enterprise.

MYTHS ABOUT HOME

1) *My child is growing up in a neighborhood.* Happily, some children do grow up in neighborhoods where there are other children to play with safely and plenty of mothers home in the afternoons to supervise them properly; but such neighborhoods are becoming rarer and rarer. Typically, both parents work until late in the afternoon or early in the evening, and many families do not have the time at home to know their neighbors well enough to join with them in a more communal effort to raise the neighborhood's children. Neighborhood institutions like the local parish church or the local grocery store have been replaced by larger "drive-to" places of worship and "super stores" in strip malls.

Thus, parents who want their children to grow up in a neighborhood environment may need to reconsider how they function as a family in their neighborhood and how their neighborhood impacts the raising of their children. Is it really the kind of neighborhood with kids playing safely together in the streets and families joining frequently for common family activities? Or is it, rather, a cluster of independent nuclear families, each distinct in its house separated by fence, yard and driveway? If the latter is the case, then parents who want their children to grow up in a neighborhood may need to go and find that neighborhood: it may well be called a boarding school.

2) *We have family dinner every night.* Again, some families still sit down to dinner together, maybe even breakfast. As Julia Child once commented, however, most Americans "graze;" we do not "eat." If both parents work or if there is only one working parent in charge of the household, the idea of sitting down to meals together becomes pretty problematical. Add the element of any kind of social life for the parents, after-school activities for the children, and the goal becomes impossible.

Ask yourself the question, "How often do we sit down to family dinner together?" Is this really something which happens properly in your family outside the weekend? Do your children behave properly? Do they speak to you and converse with you substantially about what is happening in their lives? Do they take their caps off and wash their hands to join you at the table? What are their table manners like? A 15-minute "wolf down" at the kitchen table animated by an argument about the haircut which is ended abruptly by a phone call from the girlfriend is not "family dinner."

3) *I am the best person to monitor and help my child with his or her homework.* Generally, in elementary school this is true; sometimes in middle school; rarely in high school. Two factors work against this: an adolescent's emotional need to establish more autonomy from his or her parents, and the sad reality that much of what we learned in school is now outdated. If academic work in high school is going to be substantial, then it is going to be specialized in each of the five academic disciplines of English, foreign language, history, mathematics and science. I teach history, so if a student comes to me during evening study hall with a question about history, English, French or Latin, I usually can help; but I always refer the student to the appropriate colleague if it is a question about higher algebra, calculus, chemistry or physics.

High school, as we all remember, is an emotional time, and students want to spend their time in high school emotionally bonding with each other; homework also requires time, sometimes a great deal, and teenagers often resent this. Obviously, self-motivated students usually handle this conflict very well; they find a quiet place, and they work away on their own quite happily. Many students, however, do not; and they are constantly called away by the siren call of the telephone and the television, of e-mail and the car. Parents then enter into the role of the "enforcer" and the "nag." "Have you done your homework?" becomes the defining question of the parent/child relationship. In their own defense, teenagers often don't quite answer this question honestly; parents feel betrayed. Deals are made and broken; the personal relationship deteriorates.

4) *I want my child "at home."* This assertion begs the question which is usually never asked: what does "at home" mean? Specifically, how do teenagers spend their time "at home?" Do they really spend it with their parents? Frankly, it has been my experience that being "at home" with one's parents usually means watching television, doing homework, playing on the computer and talking to friends on the phone.

As Dr. Mary Pipher argues in her book *Reviving Ophelia*, an adolescent's desire to bond with other adolescents independent of his or her parents has been enabled and empowered by modern developments in technology. E-mail and the telephone mean that they can "chill" with their friends, even when they are physically "stuck" at home; and television and the Internet mean that they also can bond with the wider, more dazzling adolescent culture beyond the home unsupervised.

Because teenagers "at home" often function in what has become an essentially autonomous adolescent culture, there is usually a scarcity of concerned, adult voices besides their parents. Teachers and coaches are relegated to specialized relationships limited to a few hours in classes and teams with large numbers of students and players. Parents, busy and distracted as they usually are, try their best to express their concerns about the precocious and narcissistic attitudes surrounding their children; but because of their isolation, they can sound different and outdated, and feel overly cautious and restricting. Parents are again the obstacle on the road to the desired end, the ones who always need explanations, but never quite "get it." Frustrated, their children often get angry or just "tune them out."

Let us consider the modern American phenomenon of the car. I am always struck by the irony of parents who plead poverty when it comes to paying a boarding tuition, but then have no trouble affording an extra car for their child to drive to school. Being baby boomers, these parents probably drove a car in high school themselves; so they see a car, I suppose, as an integral part of their child's teenage years. Certainly, it is more convenient for these parents to send their child to school in a car than to drive their child themselves; and once that pattern is established, it is rarely rescinded.

A teenager's desperate emotional "need" for a car comes at just the right time in the parent/child relationship. It comes, of course, as a gift to the parent to use as a bribe: "If you get good grades, if you behave at school, if you are pleasant in the family, . . . I will let you drive the car." What happens, of course, is that *the* car once provided soon becomes *my* car; and the struggle continues over gas money, repair bills, accidents (part of growing up), and insurance; the opportunities for parental incentive and reward, threat and punishment continue unabated.

The result, however, is that your teenager is driving "his" or "her" car not just to school, but after school and on weekends to go to the movies and to parties, or just to hang out with friends. At school, the common room becomes the parking lot, and the locker becomes the trunk. The ultimate result is that parents who choose a day school to keep their children "at home" have reduced the experience of "home" to a place for the occasional evening meal, frantic attempts at homework, and exhausted, total sleep. They keep their children "safe" by sending them out on the road to rush to school half awake in the morning and to return exhausted in the evenings if they go to a challenging school or to cruise the malls in the afternoons if they go to an easy one. Either way, "at home" for these students means "at home in the car."

CONCLUSION

If the assertions I have reviewed would be your own, and if my treatment of them has caused you to reconsider their veracity, then you may indeed be interested in a boarding school for your child. Let me just conclude by explaining that such a decision on your part will require a generous recognition of the importance of school not just in your child's education, but also in your child's development, a recognition that he or she would benefit from the direction of other adults in addition to you and that your own relationship with your child would benefit as well.

In order to make the decision to board your child, you need to be the kind of parent who is willing to "let go" a bit, to allow your child some independence and some distance from you in the community you have chosen, so that he or she can be accountable to someone else for his or her own actions and not just to you. This will require some trust on your part: trust in the school and trust in your child. You will need to let your child fall and bounce, fail and triumph as he or she grows up, stronger and wiser for the experience.

Parents who choose boarding school are choosing stronger communities in which to raise their children. These parents value community outside the home and thus value the deeper relationships with teachers and friends which stronger communities provide. These parents empower teachers to be important in their children's lives, and they empower their children to be important in their relationships with their teachers and their friends.

Boarding school then is not a replacement for your family life, but the enrichment of your family life; it is not a means to the end of college, but an end in itself, a wonderful experience of growth and adventure which should enrich your child for the rest of his or her life. It is the community, the neighborhood, the greater family which you have chosen to share with your child and to give to your child as your enduring gift.

Many Americans today view love in a very limited and limiting sense, particularly as it applies to their children and to their families. This view reflects the selfishness of our contemporary consumerist society, but it also reflects good parents' profound and understandable concern to protect and shelter their children as they grow up in a confusing and threatening world. Thus, any vehicle for love outside of the family is often viewed by parents with some suspicion. This, of course, is a shame and a hindrance, because love well offered, especially parental love, is never an either/or proposition; it is rather a both/and proposition which requires a shared response.

Boarding school then is perhaps best described as "a vehicle for parental love." It is not the only vehicle certainly, but it remains a powerful and an effective vehicle for those parents who are generous enough and courageous enough to choose it. The child who is loved by parents and school together in the stronger community which boarding alone provides is a child well raised and well educated, a child "given back" if you will; given back to his or her parents certainly, but also more importantly given back to his or her self, a self previously distracted and even alienated by the false "communities" and "neighborhoods" of our society and our time.

A Sermon
Saint James of Jerusalem: Too Glorious a Patron to be Willingly Resigned, Parents' Day Eucharist

N 1841, while he was still with Dr. Muhlenberg at College Point in New York, Dr. Kerfoot corresponded with Bishop Whittingham of Maryland about the Bishop's project of forming a church school and about the role he should play as its founding rector. In a letter dated November 3, he wrote to the Bishop about the Bishop's choice of Saint James for the name:

Right Revd. and Dear Sir,

When Mr. Lyman [the Rector of Saint John's, Hagerstown] visited us here, we thought St. James the best name we could select. Dr. Muhlenberg, however, has since urged St. Clement's Hall as preferable for sound and peculiarity. No other institution has this, while St. James is the name of a school at Bristol, PA. The high character which Scripture and pure antiquity give St. Clement is of course a great recommendation of the name. We await your approbation, and I earnestly solicit it, to prefix it to the circular, which is nearly ready. . .[1]

Dr. Kerfoot did not have to wait long, for the Bishop wrote back to him on the sixth:

My Dear Brother,

Believing that the poet's line, 'A rose by any other name would smell as sweet,' to be, by no means indifferent to the name of our establishment, I must say I am well enough pleased with that already selected (and, as I believe, published

---

[1] H. Harrison, *Life of Kerfoot* (New York, 1886) vol. i, p. 36.

*in the Church Almanac), notwithstanding its previous adoption by an insti-
tution with which ours is little likely to be confounded. Why not have both a
Pennsylvanian and a Maryland 'St. James School.' The adelphotheos (as the
Church delighted to call him) is too glorious a patron to be willingly resigned,
or for trifling reasons.*[2]

As I reread this correspondence, it occurred to me that it speaks to us today
on several levels. First, allow me to point out that there was correspondence before the telephone and before e-mail, indeed remarkably rapid correspondence,
judging from the dates of these letters. I point this out for the benefit of those
students and those parents who sometimes think that no phone means no contact: there is, in fact, a proven alternative; it is called a letter.

Indeed, I share with you the concern that those of you who will be famous (which of course will be many of you) will leave behind you no written
record of your connection with the world outside Saint James. I do not know
if the delete files in our e-mail system will still be intact; but I rather hope that
they will not, as I suspect that the dashed note sent via the Internet is not
quite as considered a document as the more careful product of pen and paper.
After all, some future headmaster may need to refer to what you have written
in order to inspire the students in some future generation at the school.

Secondly, we owe a great debt to Bishop Whittingham for saving our
name as Saint James. Imagine if he had agreed with Dr. Kerfoot to change our
name to St. Clement's. Instead of the Jacobites, we would be the Clementines,
not quite the name for a football team. As to Dr. Kerfoot's argument that
there was another school called Saint James already, I would simply make the
observation that it no longer exists. There are now other schools named Saint
James, though none I know of which are named for Saint James of Jerusalem
as we are; we may indeed be the only one.

Thirdly, and this is of particular interest to me as headmaster, we see clearly
in this correspondence between Bishop Whittingham and Dr. Kerfoot that Dr.
Kerfoot was serving the Bishop in a much larger cause. He was, as we can see, a
man under authority, deferring to the Bishop for his direction and guidance.

Saint James, you see, was founded for a greater purpose than merely educating the children in the neighborhood. It was founded to be a great church
school, a school of significance to the nation. It was founded to be itself a

---

[2] Harrison, i, p. 37.

model for a whole new kind of school, an independent school and a boarding school and a church school, pursuing a vision of community, formation, and service which would produce a different kind of alumnus, formed and intended for the good purposes of God in this world.

And we see this vision, I think, in the very name which Bishop Whittingham insisted upon giving us, because he insisted upon calling us Saint James. He insisted upon choosing for us the name of the adelphotheos as he puts it, the name in Greek for the "brother of God."

You see, the Saint James he chose for our patron was the brother of Jesus, not Saint James the apostle or even Saint James the other apostle, but Saint James the "brother of Our Lord," the other son of Mary and Joseph who saw his life transformed by the ministry and witness of his brother.

In fact, James was not even one of his brother's original followers; rather he joined the movement after Jesus had been crucified, because he came to believe in his resurrection. And because he believed in his resurrection and because he was his brother, he became himself the leader of the church in Jerusalem. Most probably private by nature, he was called to a great public ministry; certainly conservative by nature, he was called to a bold new enterprise, indeed, so bold an enterprise that it took from him his life, just as his brother had lost his life before him.

Yet, we believe that by losing his life he saved it; this is the point. This is the revelation of God that we see in Jesus Christ, in the prophets before him, and in the saints who followed after him: the way of life is love. We gain by giving, and we achieve by serving.

And this truth in which we believe stands dead set against the assumed "truth" of our time, which is the opposite: "We gain by taking, and we achieve by serving only ourselves."

Therefore, some of you who are here at Saint James may well be here under false pretenses, simply here to "get." You may be here to get a good education, to get a nice set of awards, and to get a gratifying place in a good college. You may be here for good grades without effort, honors without service, leadership without sacrifice, halls without hallmates, and rooms without roommates; in short, everything for you, yourself alone.

It is my duty to disappoint you.

For the world in this is wrong, and the truth you assume will enslave you in its falsehood. We achieve nothing good, and we certainly find no real and lasting happiness if we live just for ourselves. The truth is that the good we achieve, we achieve in this life for others, and the happiness we find, we find when we give more and more of ourselves away.

This is what Jesus Christ revealed, and this is what Saint James discovered; and this is what Bishop Whittingham wanted us to learn within the community of his school.

I am sometimes asked, "Why can't Saint James be bigger?" And the answer is that if we get too big we would lose our ability to know each other, and we would lose the imperative to love each other really in the smallness of this school. We would lose all those constant calls to sacrifice our own interests and to put the other first: to play on that team, to help that friend, to support that colleague, to take the time and to seize the occasion which could be ours and to give it to someone else.

Again, I am also sometimes asked, "Why can't Saint James be a day school? Why can't everybody go home in the afternoon and return in the morning?" But again, the answer would be the same: our community would not be as strong. We would lose the ability to gather a wider company into this school from the whole world and not just our one part of it; and we would lose the core of our society, this company of teachers and students who live together and learn to share together, not just the facts in history class or even the drill on the soccer field, but how to support a friend and how to befriend a stranger.

Yes, in many ways, Saint James would be much easier, easier I am sure for some parents especially; but it would not be the same, because it would not be as important or as demanding of self sacrifice, and thus it would lose the ability to challenge us to reach out from ourselves to others, to give ourselves to the community as a whole, and thereby to grow more fully into the likeness of God.

Two recent alumni came back to visit the other day. Successful and happy here, they have gone on to be successful and happy in college. Indeed, they attend a very fine university and are doing well. But when I asked them what was different between where they are now and Saint James, they both agreed that they found the other undergraduates to be almost comically self-promoting: bragging about SAT scores and grades on tests, insisting that difficult tasks were "easy," always anxious to show that they were as good or better than everybody else. That is what they missed the most about Saint James, they said, "We didn't do that here; we weren't like that."

And indeed they were not; they were not like that at all. Both worked very hard here, and neither was ever ashamed to show it; they shared their failures openly as well as their successes, and they found time to help their friends and then also the younger students as they grew older: students on their hall and in class and on teams with them. They did not always do this perfectly, none of us ever does; but they wanted to do this, and they found great joy in this, as they grew ever more connected to this community which they grew to love. And they were not just willing to find the time, they were also willing to set the example, to consider in their reasoning how others would be affected by what they said and did. So as a result, they made some hard decisions and denied themselves moments of popularity and pleasure in ways which most teenagers in most high schools in America are never even asked, let alone expected to do.

Therefore, as a result of their experience here, they are different. They are where they are because they have been successful as other high school graduates are successful; but unlike many who are now in college with them, they have learned a lesson here which most others have yet to learn: they have learned to live for others, and not just for themselves.

And this would be my prayer for you. I pray that each of you will learn this lesson too, and that you will emerge from this place different in just this one regard. I pray that you will learn that life is lived best for others and worst just for ourselves; because if you can learn this lesson here, then the whole of life with all its joys awaits you; and you will live in life more fully and more joyfully, as brothers and as sisters of God.

Amen.

Spring 1999

A Sermon
Preached by the Revd. Dr. D. Stuart
Dunnan at the Baccalaureate of
Washington and Jefferson College

"This is my commandment, that you love one another
as I have loved you."
John 15:12

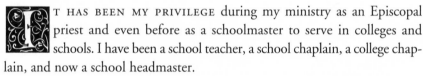T HAS BEEN MY PRIVILEGE during my ministry as an Episcopal priest and even before as a schoolmaster to serve in colleges and schools. I have been a school teacher, a school chaplain, a college chaplain, and now a school headmaster.

I use the word privilege to describe my career and my ministry, because I do think of my work as privileged in two particular aspects: first, I have enjoyed the privilege of living and working with young people between the ages of 12 and 21; and second, I have enjoyed the privilege of living and working with colleagues and students within small and well-focused academic communities like that of this college from which you now are graduating.

For instance, when I was Chaplain of Lincoln College, Oxford, I served a community of some 480 scholars (300 undergraduates, 150 graduates, and 30 fellows), and now as headmaster of Saint James, I serve a community of 240 (210 students and 30 faculty). Both communities are, of course, much larger, students and faculty constituting only the innermost of widening concentric circles. In addition to faculty and students, there are also office and support staff, alumni, and students' parents and families. In fact, some of my happiest memories of Lincoln are sitting in the medieval kitchen enjoying the company of the kitchen staff or hearing the news from a scout as she made the bed in an undergraduate's room.

My position now brings with it many varied opportunities to serve and to connect with a wide variety of people drawn by many different types of relationships into the community of Saint James School. Thus, as priest, administrator, and teacher, I myself enter into community with many different types of people in many different ways, because of my ministry and my work. Each day brings new occasions to connect: to speak in chapel, to teach in class, to make phone calls and attend meetings, certainly, but also to reach out to that student or that colleague or that parent or that alumnus in shared moments of trust and of need.

But the students are my favorites. I have to admit that. I never cease to find them interesting.

My college roommate is also an Episcopal priest, and he admitted to me once that he thought I was just a little bit "nuts" for choosing the ministry I have chosen: "You see, Stuart," he said, "you like teenagers; most people don't." Or to quote a bishop I once served who was greatly frustrated by my lack of ambition in the Church: "When are you going to graduate from high school?"

So why is it that I am so fond of teenagers? Why am I still in high school? Certainly, I would not claim that teenagers are any better as people than you or I; in fact, I admit that they are sometimes rather worse. After all, they are younger, and thus often lack the perspective and the wisdom which comes with more experience. Further, they are incredibly self-centered, and thus remarkably demanding and self-serving, often artlessly so in ways which make me cringe: mom's the housekeeper, and dad's the driver, teachers are servants, and friends are only playmates until . . .

. . . until they begin that magical transition which makes serving them, teaching and befriending them, so worthwhile: until they begin to figure it out.

You see, it is not teenagers as teenagers which makes my ministry amongst them so rewarding, it is rather what they are experiencing, their time of life, their time of transition from being recipients of love to being agents for love with and in their lives.

And this time which you have finished now, this time of college, of undergraduate experience and education, this is the time in which you should have completed this transition from being loved to loving, just as St. Claire once put it to St. Francis at the beginning of their ministry together in Assisi: "I don't want to be loved anymore; I want to love."

By the experience of living and working together at Washington and Jefferson with its particular blend of intimacy and of challenge, you should have grown towards each other here and away from your selves. You should have fallen in love here, maybe with that boyfriend or that girlfriend, but much more importantly (and probably much more permanently) with each other as friends, with your subjects and in your disciplines, with your professors and in your work. You should have completed the journey of youth here, and found in this place those purposes for yourselves which will engage you as God's instruments, His agents for Love in the world.

That is why I chose this passage from St. John's Gospel for you to hear this morning. It is, if you will, Jesus' commencement address to his disciples, his final appeal to them to live as he has lived, to continue his witness and ministry in the world. He is the vine, and they are the branches; he is God's force of love creating and redeeming in the world, and they are his chosen agents continuing his love actively and powerfully after him.

And notice to whom he speaks of love. He is not speaking to his girlfriend or even to his family members, he is speaking to his colleagues, his students, his friends: "love one another, as I have loved you."

I had a student who came to Saint James from a very close and supportive family, frankly a little too supportive. Boarding school was a bit of a shock for him, just as I am sure that college was a bit of a shock for many of you. Suddenly, he was no longer the center of attention. His mother still worshipped him, but now from afar. The most that she could do for him was to tell him that he was wonderful over the telephone and to drive the hour and half to school every weekend to tell him so in person and fetch and bring his laundry.

Rules bothered him, as they sometimes got in his way; the other students often annoyed him, as they liked to be the center of attention too; teachers sometimes failed to perceive just how special he was, and this was particularly frustrating.

But he is a good fellow with wholesome ambitions and real talent, so he began to find his way, still a little too self-centered, a little too focused on his own agenda, but earnest and admirable in his pursuits after the manner of good eleventh grade boys.

One day when we were driving to his Eagle Scout ceremony back in his home town, he asked me a question, "Father," he said, "I notice you use the word love a lot. I was taught only to use love in my family." "That's a shame," I said, "love needs to be bigger than that."

And this he began to discover to be true. As he settled further into the school and entered more deeply into his friendships, he began to have real friends, not just acquaintances and pals, but the friends who feel like brothers and sisters, friends like the friends whom I hope you have discovered here. He cried at graduation, as I hope that you will cry too.

A few months after graduation, one of these friends, really his best friend, e-mailed me. This friend is now a cadet at West Point, then in his first year, I think his first month. He wrote to tell me that this young man had written him a postcard which his corps commander had proceeded to read to the cadets. The closing led to some ridicule; because he had signed it, "love," followed by his name. I was proud of him; he had begun to figure it out.

This journey in love, this transition from being loved to loving takes us into adulthood with all the opportunities to love which being an adult can give to us.

I remember when I graduated from college and went to teach school. I felt liberated and empowered by the opportunity which teaching afforded me to teach and not just to learn, to look after my students and not just to be looked after by my teachers. It was a magical change for me, the chance at last to be important, a part of the team, to do well, to make a difference for good in actual human lives. Students from those days still write to me to keep me informed of their news: the careers they now have chosen, the families they are raising, the causes they serve. They are now important and powerful too.

Do you remember those Saturday mornings of your childhood happily settled into the couch in the family room watching cartoons in your pajamas? When did you outgrow them? When did you realize that the sun was shining outside and that there were more pressing things to do? When did you grow up? As we grow older, the "cartoons" we would watch change, and our pajamas don't have feet on them anymore, but some people still just sit around and watch them. This is how they live: they live for their pleasure and merely to avoid pain; they live alone in their laziness, simply for the moment. The world for them is two-dimensional, brightly colored and garish, never subtle in its beauty; there are no shadows, no darker hues; their lives are only superficial, because they never offer anything of themselves to others, and pain is never real.

Do not live your lives like this. Do not go forth from this wonderful college anxious to be comfortable. Rather, live your lives for real. Go forth from this place eager to be good. And not good for you either, good for the others whom God will give to you.

Our country is suffering from a lack of leadership and an absence of purpose born of our capitalist ingenuity and our material wealth. Because of the tools we have fashioned to make our lives more comfortable, we find ourselves atomized and separated from each other. Phones have replaced letters, and e-mail conversation. The friendly neighborhood market is now a huge anonymous grocery store; main street is now a shopping mall; sidewalks are broken pavement between driveways. Mom works, and dad works; and the kids are shuttled frantically from one activity to the next: "I would know you, maybe even care for you, but I can't stay."

Singles go to bars to meet other singles; couples drive great distances in opposite directions to earn the money to buy the house they barely sleep in. The family doctor has been subsumed into an HMO, the friend into the therapy group; the priest is now a psychiatrist, and lawyers argue disputes between neighbors who share a common fence.

This sad killing in Littleton and this troubling war in Kosovo also speak to me of alienation, of lives lived selfishly at a distance. These boys, ostracized, marginalized, and ignored, lashed out in rage in a high school full of strangers who commute to a huge school like workers to a factory and divide unchallenged by any kind of common culture or respected authority into homogenous, self-serving, vicious little groups. We even wage war at a distance, however noble our purpose, in "safe" impersonal ways which remove us from the conflict. We drop bombs from planes and beam pictures over satellites and write checks for homeless refugees from positions of great comfort, in no sense diminished by our token acts of charity. Where is the personal engagement in this, the commitment of our selves for others, the community born of sacrifice so strong in World War II?

Community can be found sometimes only vicariously in chat rooms and on TV. Have you ever wondered why shows like *Cheers* and *Friends* and even *Star Trek* are so popular? They offer love: the love of friends and colleagues and fellow travelers, the love which builds and sustains community. As we watch at home, we share in their love and feel a part of the group; we join in their struggles, share in their sorrows, and experience their triumphs as our own.

Typically, Americans do not live in community as we once did; we have withdrawn into our own individual domestic units. We have reduced our experience of love to familial love and romantic love; we have impoverished our experience of love to make it safe, and we have placed too much burden upon it, focused it too narrowly, so that often it just blows up. We have lost sight of that great truth about love which Jesus taught his disciples: we have forgotten that love is itself the source of life, not just love for our parents or even our children, or love for that one special person with whom we hope to have our children, but love for our work and our community, love for our friends, and love for our neighbors, even indeed love for the strangers in our world.

And there is one other love which often we forget, perhaps because it is the hardest for us to define, but most probably because it is the most challenging for us to follow. It is that love of the Greater beyond us which can transform us: the love of beauty and of truth, of honor and of goodness which calls us always to stretch ourselves to be better, to try to change for good. This is the love which counts the most, because this is the love which encourages us to make promises and to keep them, to create, to build, and to sustain with our lives. This is the love which calls us to be active and effective in purposes much larger and much more lasting than our own.

This is the love which I as a Christian priest would call the love of God, both God for me and me for God, the love with Love itself which can inspire and transform our lives. I have known this love, and I am grateful for it. I wish the same for you.

I wish you progress on the same journey of love, as each of you will walk it. I wish you many challenges and many opportunities to learn and to grow in love towards all around you, to serve others as you can serve them, to live with them in strong and real communities, to suffer as you sacrifice. I wish you lives inspired by faith and directed in prayer towards that kingdom of love for which we pray.

Gather then not for yourselves with your talents in this life, but give with your talents for others. Do what my ancestor the Revd. John McMillan who founded this college did: toil mightily to build great places, not for you, but for those whom you serve and those who will come after you. For in this way, you will continue as strong branches further along the same true vine bearing the same good fruit, fruit that lasts.

Amen.

Spring 1999

A Sermon
"Oh God . . ."

HEN I WAS GATHERING MY THOUGHTS before an alumnus' funeral recently, I found myself considering the words of the school prayer. I trust that you remember them:

Oh God, because without you we are not able to please you, mercifully grant that your Holy Spirit may in all things direct and rule our hearts; through Jesus Christ Our Lord. Amen.

For some reason, for the first time, I was struck by the opening salutation: "Oh God."

Often, Christian prayers are addressed to a person of the Trinity, most typically the person of the Father. Thus, when Christians pray, we pray into the purpose of God which is Love, this purpose uniting the three persons of the Father, Son, and Holy Spirit, creating and redeeming the world.

Thus, we pray as Jesus taught his disciples to pray, addressing the Father in the role of the Son, committing ourselves to the purpose of the Holy Spirit: "Our Father, who art in heaven, hallowed be thy name; thy kingdom come, thy will be done, on earth as it is in heaven."

We also, of course, pray to the Son, as in "Lord Jesus, stay with us, for the day is past and the evening is come;" or again, "Keep watch, Dear Lord, with those who work or watch or weep this night, and give thine angels charge over those who sleep." And we pray to the Holy Spirit: "Come, Holy Spirit, come."

The school prayer, however, does not address God through a person of the Trinity, but God as Trinity directly, skipping the nouns if you will, and going directly to the verb, the verb which we believe to be the purpose of our existence: "Oh God, because without you we are not able to please you."

Interestingly, the school hymn does the same thing. Paraphrasing the writer of the 90th Psalm, the eighteenth-century poet Isaac Watts addresses

God enthroned in all His glory: "O God, our help in ages past, our hope for years to come, our shelter from the stormy blast, and our eternal home." Here again, we have that sense of God as a redeeming and sustaining purpose in our lives, God as the permanent source and meaning for our lives, God with us and for us, just as He was with and for the saints before us.

Now, I am sure that many of you are thinking to yourselves, "What in the world is he on about? This is Alumni Weekend, for heaven's sake. He should be giving a nice sentimental sermon about teachers and friends and growing up at Saint James; instead he is getting all theological. Why is he talking so much about God?"

The answer is right here before us, staring out at us from the beginning of the school's prayer, the beginning of the school's hymn: "Oh God;" not, oh alumni, oh teachers, oh students, oh parents; but oh God. This is how we begin, this is where we look for authority and for purpose in our lives.

Now, some of you may be willing to go along with me on this, willing perhaps to concede that I might be on to something. After all, when you think about it, these words are often spoken at Saint James, even outside the chapel: frivolously and blasphemously in the phrase often repeated by teenagers in today's America, "Oh my God;" but also seriously and intentionally in many silent prayers offered from the heart.

Let us consider the prayer offered by the student before a test: "Oh God, give me an A," or even more desperately, "Oh God, help me to pass." Or again, let us consider the prayer offered during a game: "Oh God, give me this goal," or again, more desperately by the goalie, "Oh God, help me to block this goal;" "make it go in;" "make it stay out;" "give me the wings of faith to run faster than this guy behind me, the strength of Samson to hit it out of the park, the faith of Gideon to believe that we can win." Indeed, when it comes to athletics, I always think that Saint James does a particularly good job of encouraging our students to pray; it comes with our size, for we are always David against Goliath, and David had reason to pray. Without God, he could not win; and so it is with us. As Mr. Meehan always reminds his team after a hard-fought victory, "That's why we go to chapel."

And then there are prayers offered of a more personal nature: "Oh God, make her notice me," or "make him notice me;" "may she say yes," "may he say yes;" "may he never ask me at all." And there is prayer as it sometimes relates to me as headmaster: "Oh God, don't let him find out;" or "encourage him, oh God, to be merciful." Indeed, I am grateful for the continuing miracle of sight in my life, given all the prayers offered for my occasional blindness over these past seven years.

And students, of course, are not the only ones who pray like this, so do the faculty; we pray right along with our students: "help them to get it, to succeed, to win; to remember their lines, to sing their solos; to tell the truth in their moments of temptation, to choose the right and to avoid the wrong." "Give them great SAT's, oh God, and good college placement;" "preserve them from the arrogance and laziness which disrupt our classrooms and fill our work squads;" "guard them from the foolishness which leads to suspensions and dismissals;" "keep them safe, oh God, and keep them good."

And faculty pray, of course, for ourselves as well, for the patience and stamina and humility to persevere; for the wisdom we always need, but sometimes lack; the grace to repair broken relationships, the empathy to bridge the gaps which can develop between us and sometimes hinder us from helping the most needy of our students.

And parents pray too. "Oh God" is a phrase quite often on their lips, because they pray for their children and for us, as well as for themselves. They pray for the success of their children and their safety; they pray eagerly for their future, even as they pray anxiously for their present. "Oh God, help them to graduate, to win that prize, to learn that lesson, to make that goal. And give us the patience, oh God, the generosity, the wisdom, and the sanity which we will need as their parents to survive."

But you who are alumni, you offer a different kind of prayer at this altar, not so much prayer in the moment or even prayer for the future, but prayer about the past: thanksgiving, I am sure, for time spent here, now lost, but also now appreciated; friends and teachers once here with you, now separated from you, living at a distance in this world and also in the next; buildings and places on this campus now changed or even replaced with new buildings and new places not a part of your own experience at Saint James.

And you remember those prayers once offered here by you and your friends, your teachers and your parents; you remember that time of challenge and triumph, of disappointment and victory, of narrow escapes and deserved punishments, of great passion and high dudgeon, of talents confirmed and hopes dashed, of promises kept and promises broken; a time which called for prayer and taught the need for prayer, even if the motives were often selfish.

And for this reason, you have a great gift to offer to the rest of us: the perspective of time since, of lives further lived. For you can look back to your prayers and remember them with a smile, valuing the friendships and the challenges still, but seeing beyond the prayers of the moment, however desperate and heartfelt they may have been at the time, to the guiding hand of God which preserved and directed you in love all along.

So it is, perhaps, you who can tell the rest of us just what it is that the school prayer and the school hymn are about, just what it is that we are praying for: not "Oh God, help me, or even, help them to win or escape or succeed or achieve;" but "Oh God, help me and help them to become more truly and more fully yours."

For this is the purpose of our prayer and the purpose of our hymn, the point about our relationship with God which those of us who learn and grow and struggle here can often sadly forget. We are not praying to God to ask him to cheat for us on tests, or even to excuse us the consequences of our mistakes; we are not asking God to be our magical teammate or our corrupt and biased defender; rather, we are praying to God to offer ourselves to Him for His purposes however they may unfold before us in and with our lives.

This is what we ask for in our prayer, "Mercifully grant that your Holy Spirit may in all things direct and rule our hearts;" and again in our hymn, "Be thou our guide while life shall last, and our eternal home."

And this petition stands at the heart of our philosophy as a school: students should not come to Saint James expecting to get what they want, or even to learn to get what they want; they should come to Saint James expecting to learn to give themselves away. Therefore, they need to be prepared to grow and to change in surprising and transforming ways, to develop in new ways for good purposes, to embrace the challenges and disappointments which will confront them here as occasions for grace, occasions to reach out in love toward others and to grow into the likeness of Christ.

And I know that this is not the way that students always want to grow here, or the way their parents or even their teachers always want them to grow, anymore than we always want to grow in this way ourselves. But I do know that they must grow in just this way if they are going to live their lives well, dedicated to those good purposes in life which alone endure. For God is Love; and God as Love calls us forward into His own redeeming purpose, not hopelessly into some void which will consume our lives and discard our souls, but faithfully into His future, a future which can transform our lives and redeem our souls, if only we look to Him.

Whatever our talents, then, whatever our gifts, whatever our journeys—past, present, and to come—God is here before us, and God is well addressed by us in hope and in faith, for God has called us in Christ to follow in His way. Let us then commit ourselves to God anew with these words which those before us have chosen so carefully for us to pray. Let us realize what these words mean, and let us mean what they say.

Amen.

Fall 1999
_____

A SERMON
EMBRACING CHALLENGES IN LIFE,
PARENTS' WEEKEND

*Now faith is the assurance of things hoped for, the conviction
of things not seen. For by it the men of old received
divine approval.*
Hebrews 11:1–2

I HAVE BEEN THINKING ABOUT CHALLENGES RECENTLY. I have been thinking about challenges, because I am surrounded by people facing challenges; and there is a reason why I am surrounded by such people: I am the headmaster of a boarding school surrounded by young men and women growing up.

There is the successful three-sport athlete struck by a debilitating injury at the beginning of his senior year. All that he had worked so hard for, all that he had hoped to contribute and to achieve appears to him to be lost. How does he respond? How does he make the most of it? How does he meet his challenge?

There is the straight-A student who came to Saint James from a less demanding school. The As are now Bs, indeed there are even some Cs. The other students know more than she knows. What is review for them is completely new to her. They write more fluidly than she writes. They take better notes. They know what an A paper looks like; she has yet to write one. She goes to the teacher for extra help; she has never needed extra help before; she is mortified to ask for it. She is embarrassed and appalled no longer to be the "smartest" in her class. How does she respond? How does she meet her challenge?

There is the boy just dumped by his girlfriend. He thought it was "forever;" he felt it was "forever;" he invested in her as if it were forever. He removed himself from other friends, dropped other commitments; invested all his free

125

time into this one all-consuming relationship. But now it is gone. She has moved on; he is left behind. And still they are at school together; they see each other every day. Perhaps he has even been replaced, replaced even though he was once assured that "there would never be anyone else." How does he respond? How does he meet his challenge?

There is the new boarder missing home, the roommate who wants a single, the member of the choir who wanted the solo but did not get it, the mummer who wanted the part which went to someone else. There is the whole team which has yet to win a game; and there is that member of the team who feels he can help, but sits unused upon the bench. There is the sixth former who was not elected prefect and pretends not to care. There is the one less popular than she wants to be, the one not asked, the one taken for granted, maybe even the one whom the popular ones laugh at behind her back; they do not think she knows, but she does. How does each respond? How does each meet the challenges which face them in this place?

We are told the answer in the passage from the Letter to the Hebrews which we just heard read. We meet these challenges with faith, faith in ourselves certainly, but much more importantly, faith in God, which is to say faith in the loving purposes of God for us, faith in God's intention. This is the faith the writer speaks to us about: faith for the sacrifice and faith for the journey, faith to change and faith to grow, faith to offer ourselves and to be ourselves an offering to that greater purpose which alone redeems us all. It is the faith of Noah, Abraham, and Sarah, the faith of those who do not feel sorry for themselves or cling to what is comfortable, but rather reach beyond themselves for that "homeland" which we, alas, have yet to see.

And this is the faith which I would wish for every student at Saint James. Indeed, this is the faith which inspired the founding of Saint James some 157 years ago: faith in God and faith in God's good intention for us to grow stronger and braver, even as we grow more selfless and more generous in His service.

As you know, Saint James is a Church school in the Anglican tradition. Founded on the model of the great Church schools in England, we were designed to be different from the other schools in America. Specifically, we were designed to challenge our students not just to be better scholars, but to be better people, thus not just to teach our lessons in the classroom, but also on the playing field, in the dorm, and in the chapel. From our very founding, those chosen to teach in this place have been chosen to teach not just their subjects and their disciplines, but also to teach a way of life, in fact a way which we be-lieve to be the way of life: the way taught by the prophets, revealed in Jesus, and made manifest in His saints.

And yes, times have changed. Saint James is a much more diverse com-munity these days, and we are, all of us, the richer for it. We have students from every major world religion and every major Christian denomination. As an Episcopal school, we welcome them and learn from them, in countless op-portunities for mutual discovery and broadening dialogue not available to ear-lier generations. There is a greater variety of faiths within the faculty as well. Different journeys have brought each of us here to teach in this one still dif-ferent place.

For there remains, I think, one important difference about us which sets us apart still from other schools: it is our common and distinct commitment to teach the better journey in life, the better way of life to our students. We want our students to be good in those ways which we still, all of us as a fac-ulty, believe to be good. We want them to be good people who live their lives beyond this place for positive, creative purposes, serving the wider communi-ties in which they live, and living their lives selflessly for others and not just selfishly for themselves.

And this still requires just that kind of faith of which the writer speaks: faith in themselves certainly; but more than this, faith in God and faith in God's good purpose for them, changing them, stretching them, challenging them to grow better, stronger every day. And it is this faith which requires them to be challenged, because it requires them to grow in response to chal-lenge, indeed to grow up.

Young people who are not challenged to be generous remain selfish. Those not challenged to consider the needs and feelings of others (even their teach-ers) never do. Those not challenged to care for the space in which they live or the people with whom they live leave this care to someone else. Those not challenged to tell the truth when it is difficult to tell the truth will lie like five-year-olds well into adulthood, even at the highest reaches of power. Those not challenged to give to others will only expect others to give to them. It is in com-munity that we learn these things; for it is in community that we are challenged to grow in love.

Some challenges are of course particular to particular people, addressing their own special gifts and talents. The athlete is challenged to grow stronger and faster and better in her sport, the student more skilled and more thoughtful in his studies. And there are also particular challenges which come to school from home, the result themselves of the different circumstances of family life. Some students have two parents; some have one; some have four. Some have great wealth; some have very little. Some have seen the world; some have barely seen Hagerstown. Some have parents who care for them, perhaps at times too much; some have parents who ignore them.

But the real challenges, the important challenges are shared: the challenges to be good, generous, honest, loyal and brave. To shield students from these challenges, to do more than to befriend, advise and assist them as they meet these challenges, to swoop in and save them and make these challenges our own is to lose sight of the goal. For they must meet these challenges themselves if they are to grow in faith as the good result of their own struggle.

And here, of course, I have a tremendous advantage over every parent in this chapel. This is now my eighth Parents' Weekend at Saint James, and indeed my fifteenth year in service to the young. That challenge which may strike one particular student as insurmountable and therefore terrify that student's parents, I have seen surmounted many times by other students before. But more than this, I have seen the growth in faith, the growth toward strength and goodness which can and will result.

And I have learned more about faith and more about the need for challenge to elicit faith from students at Saint James than I ever learned from all my studies at Harvard or at Oxford. I am in their debt, and I am humbled by their example.

I think of the girl who came to me to resign her prefectship after her friends had convinced her to drink a beer at a party at the beginning of the summer: "Everyone will think that this is your fault, Father; but I did it, this is my fault." I think of the boy who lost too much weight for a wrestling match and lost the match after I told him he had to wrestle at the higher weight class because that was what we had originally agreed upon. "Are you mad at me?" I asked, "Did you pin me?" he asked in return. "I'm not mad at you." I think of the boy I expelled when he admitted to smoking marijuana in his dorm room. "Why didn't you lie?" I asked. "It wouldn't have been the same if I had" was his answer.

I think of the boy who came to me concerned for another boy whose father had just died. "He has it really hard, Father." This was not in itself a remarkable statement, except when you consider that this boy had lost his mother just a few years earlier. I think of the girl whose doctors told her mother that she would never walk, now playing field hockey, not the best player maybe, but perhaps the bravest. I think of the students who travel to Saint James halfway around the world at very young ages to live in a different culture and to learn in a different language, never once complaining or seeking to go home except for long vacations. I think of a boy's response when I tried to comfort him after his mother had taken her own life: "That's all right, Father, I know you're just trying to say something kind."

So yes, there are challenges in life, here at Saint James and for the rest of life too; and these challenges can feel overwhelming at times. None of us is alone in this, so we do well to reach for help and for friendship, for counsel and for understanding as we struggle to meet these challenges as our own, but we do not do well to duck them in all the ways that we are tempted to duck: to cheat, to lie, to lay the blame on someone else, or simply just to quit.

For the test of faith for each of us lies in how we meet these challenges, not just our faith in ourselves or indeed our faith in those who help us, but our faith in God and our faith in God's good purpose for us. Because however overwhelming these challenges may feel to us, they are actually only opportunities for us to grow in our response, and thus to grow into that service of God and into that likeness of Christ which our founders set before us as our first and greatest goal.

Amen.

A SERMON
WE HAVE LOST OUR BEST FATHER
CHRISTMAS, AT THE FUNERAL
OF ROBERT GRAB

"Blessed are those who mourn, for they shall be comforted.
Blessed are the meek, for they shall inherit the earth.
Blessed are the pure in heart, for they shall see God."
Matthew 5:4–5, 8

WOULD LIKE TO BEGIN MY REMARKS WITH A TRUE STORY. It is a story about Robert Grab and about Saint James School, but really, I think, a story about God. This story comes from the end of Robert's life with us at the beginning of his final struggle with his illness. It did not take place at Saint James School, rather at Johns Hopkins University Hospital, the Nelson building, the fourth floor.

As most of you know, Robert first fell ill at the beginning of February. He went to Washington County Hospital where he was treated successfully for the first effects of what turned out to be the Epstein-Barr Virus and then transferred to Johns Hopkins for further treatment and diagnosis. After some time there, he was better, so he returned to his home on campus to recuperate at the end of the month. The virus then spread to his brain, so he returned to Hopkins a week later. As I recall, his brother Charles drove him down himself.

As Sandra Pollock and I were in Baltimore for a conference at the end of that week, I went in to visit Robert on Thursday. He had become more confused by that time, though he still recognized me and greeted me with his usual warm and welcoming smile. The greeting was an effort however, and he soon fell asleep.

Alarmed, I asked to see the attending physician who graciously agreed to meet with me, but was obviously a little confused by the exact nature of our relationship. I explained that I was Robert's priest, his colleague, his friend, and that we lived in the same community. I could see that he was trying to figure out if Robert were some kind of monk, which I thought was particularly ironic, as I always thought that Robert essentially was some kind of a monk, and I often teased him about his "monkish" Friar Tuck tendencies.

I remember once that I sent Robert a brochure for aspirants to the Holy Cross Monastery, with the note, "Interested?" I looked forward to his usual gentle reprimand: "Now, Father. . . ." Instead, I had an unexpected visit from our business manager, Richard Bettencourt, who arrived at my office door somewhat exercised, pamphlet in hand, wondering whether I had something in mind for him. You see, Mrs. Youngblood had sent the pamphlet to Richard by mistake, or at least I think it was by mistake. . . .

In any case, the doctor was not at all sure that he should be telling me the details of Robert's condition until a voice came from the end of the hall: "Father Dunnan, I have always wanted to meet you. I am Vincent Liu, and I am a Saint James alumnus; I am Mr. Grab's nurse." Encouraged by Vincent, the doctor filled me in.

Vincent came from Hong Kong to Saint James School in the same year that Robert Grab became a full-time teacher: it was 1980, exactly 20 years ago. Robert taught him to play the piano, welcomed and loved him as he has a whole generation of students since. Now, Robert was with him in his place to be loved and cared for by him in return. I later asked the hospital chaplain what the chances were for such a coincidence: "One in thousands," she said.

I will confess to you that I saw the hand of God in this—God's care for such a worthy and beloved servant, the miraculous presence of his angels by human instrument, the welcome of his saints. Somehow, in God's good purpose, Saint James was with Robert in that huge and intimidating place, not following him, but greeting him; not going to see him, as I did, but there, already, to welcome and to care for him, as Vincent did on behalf of us all.

Now, I tell you this story to comfort you, to express to you my sincere and firm conviction, born of my experience, that Robert died as he lived: close to our Father, embraced by our Savior, protected and sustained by the Holy Spirit.

Indeed, this is my answer to that inevitable challenge which rises within all of us who loved Robert, my answer to the question put to me by so many students and teachers and alumni: "Why would someone so good die so young?" Even when he was with us, Robert seemed to fit God's heaven more than our earth. His humility, his gentleness, his patience, his generosity, his faith: in all these ways, he was different from the rest of us; no, let us admit it, he was better. There is this sense in which I think all of us who knew him well shared, even when he was healthy and jolly and funny, this sense that he was better than this world, perhaps just visiting, belonging really to the next.

And yes, God makes his rain to fall on the good and the bad alike. We all suffer; we all die; and some of us die young. The question for us in this life then is How do we live? or even better, For what do we live?

The answer in Robert's case is as clear as it is enduring. He lived for beauty, and he lived for love. He lived for the beauty he created with his remarkable talents as a musician. His skill as a trumpeter was surpassed only by his gracious willingness to play on the stage and in the band certainly, but also in just about every church in Washington County and in every nursing home and school. Did you ever know Robert Grab to say no? Did you ever know him to refuse, because he was too busy or the fee was too low or the audience beneath him?

In a world of prima donnas and self-centered "artistes," Robert Grab, like his brother Charles, stood out as a generous and humble craftsman who produced real art with hardly any ego or any ego need. He was, I suppose, the true trumpeter who used his talent to support the overall sound from the back of the orchestra, to play fanfares for others, and never for himself.

And he sang in the same way. He sang beautifully in that natural and steady tenor which straining baritones, like me, can only envy. And again, he sang selflessly in the back, supporting the whole choir with the strength of his voice and the skill of his musicianship. As a soloist, he sang again to support the liturgy, never to upstage it. He sang because he loved music, and he loved to sing to God.

It is in this capacity that Robert will be especially missed at Saint James: his steady leadership in the choir and at Compline on Sunday nights, but most especially on Friday mornings at the "holy hit parade" in chapel. On Fridays, he led the whole school with enthusiasm, seeking to inspire reluctant and occasionally sullen teenagers to shake their lethargy, to lose their debilitating anxiety for "coolness," to just lift up their hymnals and sing.

Finally, and this is perhaps appreciated best by us who knew him at school, Robert was a creative and enthusiastic gardener who found his greatest joy working with Mr. Hoyer and with a steady succession of varsity groundsmen in the school's gardens. Again, he was generous and selfless with his treasure and his talents. He gave countless hours of hard work and often bought the plants and supplies with his own money. Even his garden at Ferguson House remains after him as his own beautiful gift to the school.

Perhaps Robert's finest moments of artistry came twice a year, at Christmas and at Easter, when he brought his love of flowers and of music together into this chapel. By his genius and with his selfless, substantial effort, this sacred space was filled with the beauty of cedar trees and poinsettias in the winter and lilies and daffodils in the spring. Choir and brass rejoiced at our Lord's birth and resurrection in glorious pageantry and in song. Even the linens on the altar were ironed by his hand.

It is, therefore, particularly appropriate that Robert should be buried from this chapel, for he loved it and cared for it as his spiritual home. He has cared for every brick in this place, tended every candle, and maneuvered a succession of priests into the ways of reverence and of prayer which he inherited from Father Owens and preserved for him unbroken. It has been strange indeed to walk into the sacristy and not find him there, to go to the Mary Chapel and find that the lamp of the tabernacle has lost, with him, its oil.

A student told me the other evening that he had decided that Mr. Grab was irreplaceable. I asked him why. "Because Mr. Grab's job was really to be Mr. Grab."

Saint James is a busy place, but Robert was never too busy to listen. Saint James is a school dedicated to achievement and excellence, but Robert never really cared how you did; he just loved you. In the chapel and in the dining room, in the library and at home for one of his famous open houses, Robert created his own room with his presence, his own emotional space. All were welcomed there, all were appreciated, all were understood, whether it be the student in trouble or the teacher frustrated or even the headmaster harassed, we all knew where to go and to whom to talk.

So we shall miss him. We shall miss this kind and generous man who stayed and loved this community as others moved on through it, who cared for its special places and preserved its holy purpose, who included the marginalized and embraced the outcast. We shall miss his presence with us, and we are challenged by his absence from our company. We are challenged, I think, to be now ourselves that much more generous, that much more humble, that much more thoughtful and kind.

Perhaps God has chosen to welcome Robert home a bit earlier as a challenge to us all: no longer to count on Robert to do for us the good which we can do ourselves; to be, in short, more like Robert, and thus more like that true and faithful disciple whom Jesus calls us to be in his beatitudes, to find our blessings in simple acts of giving and our purpose in God's enduring momentum of love.

On behalf of the School, I cannot begin to express to Charles and Denise, their children, and to all of Robert's family the depth of our sympathy at their loss. The man we loved as teacher, colleague and friend, they loved as brother, uncle and nephew. He loved his family deeply, and his family loved him. I know from this shared time with them that Charles and Denise could not have been more attentive nor more faithful to their brother, and I know I speak for all of us when I thank them for their courage and their faithfulness.

All of Hagerstown, indeed this whole county, will feel this loss. Wherever we gather to create fine music, to enjoy real fellowship, and to pray in faith, Robert will be missed. We have lost our best Father Christmas; let us find him in ourselves. My hope is that we can, and my hope has been strengthened by the tremendous response of love elicited by Robert's journey home.

Just yesterday morning, it fell to me to lead the holy hit parade in Robert's place. We sang four of the hymns which we are singing this morning, and I have never heard the students produce a more vigorous nor a more beautiful sound. Frankly, they needed to, because most of the faculty (including me) were crying.

I saw great significance in this. You see, in the end, God, through Robert, got his wish; they just lifted their hymnals, opened their hearts, and sang.

Amen.

A Sermon
Our Journeys in Life,
Alumni Weekend

*By faith Abraham obeyed when he was called to go out to a place
which he was to receive as an inheritance; and he went out, not
knowing where he was to go."*
Hebrews 11:8

JOHN KEBLE WAS PERHAPS THE MOST ADMIRED FIGURE in his
generation at Oxford University. He "came up" to the University by
winning a distinguished scholarship and graduated with the highest
honors in 1811. He went on to become a fellow of Oriel College and the University Professor of Poetry. Ordained a priest in 1826, he was remarkably de-
vout for his time. His collection of spiritual poems titled *The Christian Year*
was published many times and widely read throughout the English-speaking
world. We find his words in our hymnal today and also poignantly on the
gravestone of the two-year-old Sarah Passmore who died in 1856. Her tablet
is against the stone wall above the football field, and it proclaims in Keble's
words that she is "safe in the saints above."

At Saint James, we should especially remember John Keble as one of the
principal leaders of the Oxford Movement whose American followers, William
Whittingham and William Augustus Muhlenberg, founded Saint James in
1842. Most notably, it was Keble who mounted the pulpit of St. Mary the Vir-
gin in 1834 to preach his now famous "Assizes Sermon" on "National Apostasy"
challenging the Rationalist assumptions of his generation and calling for a re-
newed, more vigorous Church of England.

I thought of John Keble at the end of March, first because his feast day
is on the 29th and second because of Robert Grab's funeral on the 25th.

Witnessing that impressive event on campus and welcoming that large company of some 600 mourners who came, many a great distance, all on two days' notice, I was reminded of a story told from John Keble's funeral.

Unlike most Oxford fellows who were ordained just to be eligible for their fellowships, Keble took his ordination seriously, and resigned from all his University offices to serve as a parish priest in the country. In 1836, he became the vicar of the little church at Hursley near Winchester, and he served there for the remaining 30 years of his life.

When he died, there was a large gathering of famous and important leaders in the Church and in society who came to his funeral, including Prime Minister Gladstone who had admired Keble when he was an undergraduate. Witnessing this remarkable event, his parishioners were surprised, for they had no idea that this man whom they had known for 30 years as their faithful and gentle pastor was in fact so famous. The story is told of one old farmer in the village who asked a newspaper reporter, "Why have all these great men come to see good Mr. Keble buried?"

And so it was with Robert's funeral, who was himself inspired by Keble's spiritual writings and example; the many came to honor the one, and the great gathered to honor the good. And so also last night when we gathered to honor Chick Meehan for his many years of selfless and loyal service to Saint James, the many came to honor the one, the great gathered to honor the good.

The passage from the Epistle to the Hebrews which we just heard read speaks of a journey, the journey of Abraham, called "to go out to a place which he was to receive as an inheritance. And he went out, not knowing where he was to go." People do a lot of that these days. They gather up their lives, and they head off on journeys. We live in a time of easy mobility and in a culture of fluid opportunity, and we are constantly encouraged to "move on" and "move upwards."

Indeed, this pattern of moving to achieve begins in that bold first journey to college which our sixth formers are just now anticipating. Their time of preparation in this place will soon be over; the time has come for them to journey to that next place which is, despite their best efforts and the best efforts of their parents (not to mention our college counselors), largely still unknown. They journey forth to somewhere new to advance themselves and to further their careers, to build, in short, their futures. And this journey will bring, in four years, a new journey: to graduate school or to that first job, and then on to the next job or indeed (my sympathies to any parents attending) graduate school again.

Both Robert Grab and Chick Meehan made this same journey when they were 18 years old, Chick from the dormitories of Saint James School and Robert from his parents' farm down the road. They both graduated, and they both returned; and they both then stayed. But theirs, alas, is no longer the usual pattern.

I say alas, because the schools we serve have become less stable as a result of our increased mobility, and thus at risk of losing the more faithful witness and more powerful sense of community which our staying can provide. And schools are not alone in this. In all the ways that we live and serve together, in our work, in our neighborhoods, and in our family life, this "up and away" attitude brings a more constant sense of disruption, vulnerability, and loss than was true in the past.

I also say alas for ourselves, because we are now all too tempted to flee the challenges which face us when we stay and to move on to that magical, better place where we will be happier, more successful, more appreciated and more important. Like a child sent to his room whose room becomes "better anyway" or the friend rejected who finds "new friends who like her better," we sometimes fail to address what is wrong within us and flee to avoid the challenges without.

Jesus reminded us that a prophet is without honor in his own country, and we all experience this lack of appreciation every day. I, myself, often point out to the students that at some schools headmasters are treated with respect. Their response is a good one: "Yes, Father, but not always with affection like you." The people who really know us usually take us for granted, laugh at us too much, forget to thank us, and often ignore us. This can be maddening, even hurtful, and the easy solution is a tempting one: leave. "They will know the difference once I have left them."

The reality is that "they" will not; "they" will just move on themselves, continue along their own foolish path and take the one who replaces us for granted, too. We, in turn, soon discover that honored as we were by those who welcomed us, we are now taken for granted again, just as we were before; "they" are still the problem, failing to honor us as the true prophets that we know ourselves to be. Time to "move on" we say, time to find that "better" place.

But the cause for all of this false, retreating movement lies within ourselves; it lies in that false, sinful distinction which we make in our hearts between "I" and "them." This is why John Keble left his glory at Oxford behind him and journeyed to that parish in the country, and this is why he stayed. In his self-giving care for his people, he lost the "I" exalted, and joined with "them" in a new "us."

The point about the sorrow we shared at Robert's funeral and the laughter we shared at Chick's roast is the same: we shared it. We shared a feeling of connection and community born of our common association with these good men over 20 and 31 years. And we shared this feeling, because they provided themselves to us and stayed with us, linking friends to friends with their presence, even generations to generations. This was Robert's home; this is Chick's home; and this is "our" home with them together.

Now obviously I recognize that the realities of our time are as they are and that it is only appropriate that young people advancing in their careers and older people whose tasks are accomplished move on for their own benefit and for the benefit of the communities they serve. Certainly, in the continuing journeys of our lives, we often grow with change in our environment and the assumption of new duties. Similarly, our communities also grow with the new ideas, assumptions, and personalities which those who replace us bring with them.

But there needs to be a better balance within us if we are to live in this age of greater mobility more faithfully, a more thoughtful approach to moving in our lives and a more selfless commitment to staying in our communities. We will all move and stay as we progress, but we need to move and stay for the right reasons, reflecting a more faithful commitment to the one true journey which must and should inspire us.

And what is this journey? It is not the physical journey of moving or staying in this world, but the spiritual journey which directs us towards the next. It is the journey that the writer to the Hebrews tells us about in his epistle, the journey of John Keble and all the saints, their journey in imitation of Christ, their journey towards holiness, towards service, towards usefulness, their journey home to God.

And yes, this journey sometimes requires us to move on, just as it sometimes requires us to stay put, and both can be emotionally challenging; but the spiritual imperative of our faith requires that we make our decisions for the good, not just for our own good, but for the good of those we serve. Certainly, it is difficult for us to discern at times which we should do, but that is why God has given us minds to think and hearts to pray. For whether we move or stay physically, we are always journeying spiritually, and there is, in the end, only one purpose which this journey requires. It requires love, not love for ourselves, but love for the others, even the very ones who take us for granted and fail to honor us, who laugh at us and enjoy us, who know us and care for us, and are the better for our time with them.

For this good purpose, God has given them to us. He has placed them with us as the surprising but true objects of our challenging but possible faith. And He has placed further on before us a better place at the end of our pilgrimage which we can already share and create in love together, not a place we can always see or even always appreciate, but still a place we can feel and know in our hearts as real and true and lasting.

Amen.

A Sermon
Preached at St. Mark's Parish,
Locust Street, Philadelphia

*Jesus answered, "The first is, 'Hear, O Israel: the Lord our God,
the Lord is one; you shall love the Lord your God with all your
heart, and with all your soul, and with all your mind, and
with all your strength.' The second is this, 'You shall love
your neighbor as yourself.' There is no other commandment
greater than these."*
Mark 12:29–31

N THE PORTION OF ST. MARK'S GOSPEL assigned for this morning, we hear again Our Lord's famous summary of the Law in his
response to the scribe's question, "Which commandment is the first
of all?"

Predictably, Jesus repeats the Shema, the traditional summary from
Deuteronomy 6:4 which the Jews repeated daily as a pledge of their allegiance
to the one God of Israel, distinguishing them as it did from all the other nations in the Roman world. "Hear, O Israel: the Lord our God, the Lord is
one; you shall love the Lord your God with all your heart, and with all your
soul, and with all your mind, and with all your strength." Less predictably,
Jesus then adds the commandment from Leviticus 19:18. "You shall love your
neighbor as yourself."

By putting these two commandments together, Jesus is combining into
one commandment the call of Moses and the message of the prophets. The
faithful are made distinct by their obedience to the one God and holy to Him
by their devotion to their neighbor.

The scribe is impressed. "You are right, Teacher; you have truly said that
'He is one, and besides Him there is no other'; and 'to love Him with all the

heart, and with all the understanding, and with all the strength,' and 'to love one's neighbor as oneself'—this is much more important than all whole burnt offerings and sacrifices."

And so they agree, the scribe and Jesus. They agree on the whole purpose of God's revelation of Himself to Israel. They agree on the true meaning of God's call to us; they agree on the purpose of the Law and of all true religion. And this should not be so remarkable to us, for this is the clear message of all the Gospel narratives: Jesus came to us, confirming the pre-existing message of the prophets. God's people are called to be set apart as belonging to God not by their great power or by their great wealth, but by their great holiness. And this holiness is to be found not in public prayer and cultic sacrifice, but by a different way of life, by living not at the expense of our neighbor but in service to our neighbor, by entering into the purpose of God which is love for His creation.

And when Jesus sees that the scribe understands this, when he sees that this good man can see the way of life ahead, he reveals to him the true nature of his own divine authority, and he welcomes him: "You are not far from the kingdom of God." After that no one dared to ask him any question. For you see, after that, there is nothing left to ask.

We have two twin girls at Saint James, now in the ninth grade, and they have been with us since the seventh. One girl was born with a slightly disfigured face and significant hearing loss. She was also born brilliant, and she has been the top student in her class throughout her time with us. The other girl is very pretty and talented, a little more social than her sister, but bright as well. Sweet, good and full of enthusiasm, they could not be nicer girls, and reflect, I think, the good nature of their parents.

The family is local and Jewish, so the girls celebrated their batmitzvah together at our local synagogue two summers ago, and I was invited. They invited all their teachers and friends, and read and sang their passages with aplomb. The most moving part of the celebration came after the service when their parents spoke to them of their pride in them and their love. Given the challenges the one has faced, and the challenges the other has faced in relationship to her, the proud and loving words of their mother and father were especially moving.

However, one thing that their mother said to them surprised me and caught my attention. She reminded them that all four of their grandparents, both her parents and their father's parents, were Holocaust survivors. As I looked at these two beaming young women standing confidently at the front of the congregation, I was stunned and sickened. How could such evil happen to such good people at other people's hands?

At a later bar mitzvah for a different student also in the same temple, I happened to sit at the same table with the girls' paternal grandparents. Always the history student, I asked them to tell me their story. The grandmother was born in Hungary and the grandfather in Slovakia. They were both sent as teenagers to Auschwitz towards the end of the war, and then escaped from work gangs about a year or so later when they were working outside the camp. They met later in Prague, moved to Israel, then Cleveland, then Hagerstown where they founded the first and only dialysis center in our part of the country.

Theirs was a remarkable story, and I asked them to tell it to my advanced placement European history students at the end of the year. This they did, bravely and simply, and we all just listened to them, awed and amazed, incredulous at what had happened to them at the hands of their neighbors, and humbled by their brave resilience and generous good will.

These good people who were stolen from their families at the height of their youth and abandoned by their neighbors, who were tortured and brutalized for nothing they had done, whose relatives were killed like animals, could sit in front of us with no malice in their hearts. Indeed, they told us that the reason they came to Hagerstown was to answer the needs of those who suffered. And this, they have done for thirty years with meticulous care and loving devotion; they even refuse to retire.

Like the scribe in the presence of Jesus, none of us had anything to say. There was nothing left to say. The truth of God was there before us, smiling at us kindly in their faces. We were awed, and we were challenged.

Surely, we make our faith too complicated. Jesus didn't. He made it very simple. He taught us, and he showed us in his own sacrifice just how it is that we should live our lives. We should love God with all our hearts, and we should love our neighbors as ourselves.

As those invited by Him to enter into the life of God Himself, we are called by Him to be different, separate from the world, rejecting its greed, its hate, and its fear, but also active in the world, changing it for the good, empowered by the Holy Spirit to serve in God's good purpose. This is what it means for us to believe in the Gospel. We believe that God is Love, and believing this, we live for love and as love in the world.

A former student invited me to his graduation from Gettysburg College, because Bill Cosby was the speaker. In his speech, Mr. Cosby told a story, and as it is a Philadelphia story, I would like to repeat it to you this morning. One day when Mr. Cosby was an undergraduate here at Temple, he realized that he had locked himself out of his parents' house, so he went to his grandmother's to borrow her key. Pleased to see him, she asked him what he had done in college that day, and he told her all about his philosophy class.

"It was great," he said. "We had a big debate on whether a glass half full is really half empty." "Well, that's easy," she replied, "it depends upon whether you are drinking or pouring." The clever college boy was humbled. "She got it just like that," he told us, "only an eighth grade education, and she got it just like that."

So should we. There are just two types of people in this world; the ones who live their lives on the take, and the ones who live their lives on the give. Sometimes people on the take can be pretty bold about it, and we can identify them as evil. Such were the people who brutalized my friends. But usually people on the take are not evil so much as selfish, lazy, fearful. They are people just like us, indeed sometimes they are us.

For indeed, many people who live their lives on the take are what we would call good people. They are industrious and law abiding, scrupulously fair in their approach to life. But they are not generous, and they are not genuinely kind. They do not give, except to receive; and they do not care about anyone beyond their immediate families or their immediate circle of friends. "Good" as they often are and pleasant as they often can be, they are damned. They are damned to be forever on the take and never really on the give; damned, therefore, never to know that true happiness which comes only when we give ourselves to others; damned never to feel the great power of God to heal, to forgive, to care, to welcome, and to use us as His instruments. Yes, they are careful and they are comfortable, but they are far from the kingdom of God.

In these six days between All Saints Day and Election Day, let us consider the contrast. On one hand, the saints challenge us in this life with the enduring sacrifice of their lives, and they pray for us from heaven to join them in God's purpose. On the other hand, our politicians, in this the most wealthy and powerful country in the history of the world, play on our fears and appeal to our selfishness. Let us just consider the two major party nominees for president, as one of them is about to be elected Emperor of the Western world. Which is the candidate who calls us to give of ourselves and to help our neighbor? My conclusion would be neither. Maybe one does in some parts of his message and the other in some parts of his, but the overall message of both of them is "let me help you take." Indeed, if I understand them correctly, this is the essential debate between them: they are arguing as to which one of them can help us to take the most.

Now, we could blame them for this, or we could blame the "system," but they are, after all, only doing their jobs, telling us what we want to hear. So perhaps we need to blame ourselves and to take stock of ourselves as Christians, as followers of Christ in this age. Perhaps the time has finally come for us to listen to the one we don't want to hear, the one who tells us the Truth, simple and challenging as it is.

Are we really faithful to Him? Or are we still too selfish? How close are we to the kingdom of God?

Amen.

A Sermon
The True Victory,
Preached at Saint John's
Episcopal Church, Hagerstown

*Pilate asked him, "So you are a king?" Jesus answered, "You say
that I am a king. For this I was born, and for this I came into
the world, to testify to the truth. Everyone who belongs to the
truth listens to my voice."*
John 18:36–37

S I THINK ALL OF YOU KNOW BY NOW, I grew up in Washington,
DC, and attended school at Saint Albans, the Cathedral school for
boys. I left Washington when I went to college some 22 years ago,
and I can't help but reflect on how much Washington has changed since my
childhood. It is a much more urban and sophisticated place than it was then,
and it also appears to me to be much more affluent and more openly dedicated to the pursuit and exercise of power.

I see this every time I drive in on Massachusetts Avenue, by my old neighborhood in Westmoreland Hills, through Spring Valley, up to Ward Circle,
and then on to the Cathedral, retracing the route my father used to drive us
to school. Smaller houses have been torn down and replaced by small palaces,
open parks by gated townhouse developments. Spring Valley looks like Bev-
erly Hills, and Mass. Avenue, above Ward Circle, looks like the Upper East
Side of Manhattan.

I see this also when the Saint James teams play in games against our independent school rivals in the Washington area, particularly in boys' sports.
The play is often remarkably aggressive and the coaching unsportsmanlike. In
soccer, particularly, where the teams are well matched and the parents are al-

most always present in force, the Washington teams play to win, and they can be obnoxious about it. Certainly, there is a push to achieve and an achievement of excellence which is commendable, but there is also something else— a "take no prisoners approach" to sport, which tells me something about the attitude at home and the culture at work: only losers lose, and only winners win.

Now part of this "winner take all" attitude can be attributed to the media and the increasingly commercialized nature of professional sports on television. The television cult of the star athlete who earns tons of money and shows tons of attitude to foe and fan alike has certainly infected our culture. Now every high school basketball player wants to hog the ball and rack up the points in order to be noticed by the college scout who will give him a free education and a future shot at the NBA. Even Tiger Woods, nice man that he is, dropped out of college in order to earn more money, not just for himself but for the entire golfing industry. In our new richer and better America, we have embraced a national cult of the winner which is as pervasive as it is insidious. Remember the Olympics? Or better yet, do you remember how the Olympics were reported? Why is it that we always need to know how many gold medals America won compared to Russia, China and Germany? What difference does it make? Why is our media so disappointed when the hyped-up American sports star only wins a silver? Why is that athlete suddenly a "loser?" I don't know about you, but if I had been asked to go to the Olympics and was judged the second best in my sport in the world, I would not be a "loser."

This is always the great American question: Who will win? All the hype around the Super Bowl and the World Series manipulate us in the same direction; in between the commercials, the drama builds on our screens before us: Who will win? And this simplistic winner/loser view of life is not restricted to sports either. We have applied it to film and to science, too: Who will win the Oscar? Who will win the Nobel Prize? And we apply it to our own struggles: Who will win the contract? Who will win the promotion? Who will win the lawsuit? It is all about winning and losing.

Interestingly, this American propensity to reduce all of life's struggles to winning and losing can even warp our view of the world. There is nothing our media like more than a good quick fight. Have you ever noticed how when stories start to get a little too complicated or too foreign and there is no clear winner or loser, or no clear good side or bad side, then our attention starts to wander? Fortunately for the newscasters, there is always a new fight to claim our attention. Now we are focused on the Palestinians and the Israelis, but whatever happened to the fight in Bosnia? in Kosovo? in Iraq? These fights continue, but they have become too complicated; there is no clear winner to claim our attention, so we have moved on.

This false, oversimplified understanding of life also warps our view of history. For instance, when I teach the Dutch War of Independence against the Spanish during the sixteenth century to my European history students, I always point out to them that the Dutch national anthem to this day is a letter of surrender written by William the Silent to the King of Spain. Mystified, my students ask me why the Dutch would sing such a humiliating text as their great national song.

The point, I tell them, is not that the Dutch lost, but that the Dutch struggled as a small nation in a Europe controlled by great nations and that they would continue to struggle for the rest of their history. I point ahead to the Second World War when the Netherlands were occupied by the Nazis. Their anthem reminded them in their ordeal that this was not the first time that they had suffered for their freedom and that the struggle itself was the true test of their character and of their desire to become free again and to remain free as a full and sovereign nation.

"Oh," they say, still mystified. I can see it in the expressions on their faces; they are not at all convinced. The Dutch would not be free if "we" had not freed them. "We," the "Americans," we are the winners.

The same goes for the British. "They" would have been conquered too, if "we" the winners had not gone over and saved them. And again, I try to point out to them that in many ways the British actually won the war for us, by fighting so bravely alone after the defeat of France and before our own full entry into the War almost three years later. They still are not convinced. The British may have "survived," but they did not "win." We won; we are the winners. We won the war for them. Distressingly, they even have more admiration for the Germans during the War than the French, because the Germans beat the French. The French are the real "losers." What about the fact that the Germans fought in an evil cause? They still are not moved. At least the Germans did not lose in a couple of weeks like the French did.

If you were to delve into the media-manipulated minds of most young Americans today, you would find this one common national myth: we are the winners, and winning is everything.

And so, it appears in politics, for now we can watch this sad spectacle in Florida. It is like a close soccer match poorly refereed. One side wants these votes counted, but not those; the other side wants the opposite. One side wants recounts in some counties; the other side wants recounts in other counties. The side which is winning is pointing to the clock; the side which is losing wants overtime. Both are crying foul, both are quoting "the rules," both are yelling at the referees. And the media love it, because it's a fight, and there is going to be a winner and a loser, the great American paradigm for life

But we know there is a different paradigm, a different way to understand life and all the struggles which life will bring to us. And this is to understand life, not in terms of who wins and who loses, but who remains faithful and who proclaims the truth.

I think I have mentioned to you before a movie called *The Mission* which came out about fourteen years ago. Our fourth formers are all required to watch it as part of their developing nations course. It is the story of a papal envoy sent to the border region between Spanish and Portuguese America in the eighteenth century to close a mission run by the Jesuits who were serving the Indians and protecting them from the European slavers. In the end, the envoy does his duty; the mission is closed, and the Indians are enslaved.

As I walked out of the movie with a group of friends, they all declared it depressing. "Really?" I asked. "I thought it was inspiring." "How could you possibly have found that movie inspiring? The bad guys won, and the good guys lost."

"Yes, but weren't you inspired by that scene where the faithful priest holds up the monstrance containing the consecrated host, the broken and given body of Christ? Like Christ himself he stands bravely for the truth of God and offers himself for that truth, even dies for it."

"Yes, but he lost," they said. "The bad guys won." What part of the plot did I not understand? It all comes down to winning and losing.

"No," I said, "the bad guys only appeared to win. In the end, the truth is still the truth. Winning isn't the end, neither is losing. The truth is the end."

Is not this Our Lord's challenge to Pilate? Does he not point out to him that he did not come into the world to win, but to reveal. He did not come into the world to win power for himself but to reveal the power of God to use us for His glory in the world. He came then not to win, but to be faithful, and by being faithful, to reveal the better purposes of God for us all in the world.

Now, I am not saying that we should not strive to win in sport, in politics or indeed in all the struggles of our lives. All who know me well know that I am a very competitive person. I do not go to a game to cheer for us to lose.

But what I am saying is that we should keep our struggles in perspective, and that we should strive always to win and to lose faithfully. For we, as Christians, are called in Christ not just to be winners, but to be revealers, and not just revealers of our truth, but of God's.

Eventually, if not soon, either Mr. Gore or Mr. Bush will win; the other will lose. And when this happens, the greater opportunity for patriotism will actually come to the loser. Let us hope that he is up to it, for it is the loser who will need to end the fight and to end the fight graciously for the sake of the nation. And the winner will need to win graciously, too; frankly, he will need to win humbly, fully accepting that he did not win the clear victory that he will want to claim. Both men will be challenged to show us just how much they love this country, and thus just why it is that they have tried so hard to win our trust.

And so it is for us in our struggles. We do not always win either; sometimes we lose. But win or lose, the opportunity comes to us always at the end of the contest to give the glory to God and to offer ourselves to our neighbor, even the very neighbor who has struggled so hard against us.

You see, the true achievement of America in the Second World War was not just that we won, but that we won in the right cause, and further, that we won generously, reaching out in friendship to the very Germans and Japanese who had struggled so murderously to destroy us and our allies. This is why we are at peace, and this is why our enemies are now our friends.

Despite all appearances to the contrary, the world does not always belong to the winners in this life; it belongs to God. And the truth about God which Christ lost his life to reveal to us is that God is Love and calls us as His children to love each other. In the end, that is all there is for us to believe, and that is all there is for us to strive for.

Amen.

A Letter to Alumni,
Past Parents, and Friends

A S MANY OF YOU WILL HAVE READ IN THE NEWS, a former employee of Saint James School has been arrested on charges of child abuse stemming from his relationships with two students during his time at Saint James.

The Reverend Kenneth Kirk Behrel served as chaplain at Saint James from September 1980 until June 1985; he left Saint James because of liturgical differences with the headmaster, and has served as a parish priest in the Diocese of Chicago for the last sixteen years. As you know, I came to Saint James in July of 1992, so I did not serve with him, and I have never met him.

In March 1998, I received a phone call from an alumnus who informed me that he had been abused by Father Behrel when he was here as a student. In our conversation, the alumnus assured me that no one else at the school knew of this relationship and that he was calling me to help him make contact with Father Behrel and to help the police in their investigation. I, of course, was anxious to help him in every way that I could, providing him with Father Behrel's present address, providing all pertinent records to the police, and reporting the accusation immediately to the Diocese of Chicago. As a result of their investigation, the police discovered that there was another alumnus who reported being abused, and a Washington County grand jury issued indictments on both charges. According to the press, when Father Behrel was arrested in Chicago earlier this week, the police found cocaine and unregistered firearms in his apartment.

Because of the changes in personnel which happened before I came and then again after I arrived, Saint James is a very different place today than it was sixteen years ago, and no member of the current administration or faculty has any personal or professional connection with Father Behrel. Nonetheless, when I spoke to the school in chapel, I explained to our students that this news, shocking as it is, did not come as a surprise to me, as we have been helping with the investigation since I was first informed three years ago.

Any news story which involves moral turpitude on the part of a teacher or a member of the clergy (in this case both) is of great interest to the public at large, because teachers and clergy are rightly held to the highest code of personal and professional conduct. There is, therefore, great interest in this story in the press, and I am sure this interest will continue as the case develops through the months to come. Obviously, our obligation is to help to discover the truth and to support any who may have suffered at the hands of someone they had trusted in their pursuit of closure and of justice. My particular hope is that any alumni who may feel angry or alienated from Saint James because of such behavior in the past will feel encouraged, supported, and welcomed by our open and vigorous response in the present.

All I can do further is to assure you that we as a faculty are very mindful of your trust in us and thus of our professional and moral responsibility to protect and nurture our students. I can also assure you that I am especially mindful of my own responsibility as headmaster to make sure that we do.

Yours faithfully,

The Revd. Dr. D. Stuart Dunnan
The Headmaster, Saint James School

An Essay
The Good Mother

written for Parenting Teens: Collected Essays by Independent
School Educators

ER SON CAME TO SAINT JAMES IN THE NINTH GRADE. Intelligent, charming, good-looking and athletic, he made friends quickly and was naturally a center of attention. He also was impulsive and often lacked focus, reflecting his diagnosis of Attention Deficit Disorder. He struggled academically, but persevered. His grades for the final trimester reflected his hard work and achievement.

The mother was proud of him; her son had settled into boarding school life and had begun to focus on his studies. She delighted in his good relationships with teachers and friends, and cherished the school as "perfect for him." It also was perfect for her. She enjoyed coming to school to watch him play soccer and lacrosse, and to attend special events and services in the school's chapel. She was developing friendships of her own with teachers and other parents. The school was becoming hers in all the right ways just as it was becoming his. The trajectory was good.

Her son returned to Saint James the next year. One evening during study hall, he invited me into his dorm room. He was pleased to see me, welcoming me enthusiastically. Skiing posters adorned the walls, and the room was generally neat. He was writing an English essay on his computer.

"Hey, Father, did you see my fish?"

I paused to admire the fish tank, bubbling with clear water and the bright garish colors of cichlids.

It is amazing how fast an adolescent life can change. A few days later, he began to "go out" with an older girl who brought him into a different circle of friends: ones who like to take risks. Soon, his grades declined. His look changed, and he appeared to be more moody, preoccupied. He had less time for his friends, his teachers, and his sports. The trajectory was not good.

Seeing these things and becoming concerned, I stopped by his room one evening during study hall. The posters had changed, and the room was darker, more cluttered, and more cramped. He seemed worried to see me, and he quickly covered his computer screen to hide what he was writing. The fish tank smelled foul and was full of algae; the cichlids were gray and barely moving.

I told him of my fears, pointing to the decline in his grades and the changes in his appearance and attitude. I also noted the reputation of his friends. Speaking bluntly, I told him I suspected marijuana use. He admitted that my concerns were justified, but assured me that he was not smoking pot. Maybe his friends were, but not he. We came to an awkward silence. He had rejected my offer to help, telling me only part of the truth. I left him that night feeling something more of a stranger.

One week later, the hall master was investigating some noise after "lights out" in a boy's room. He smelled smoke, and discovered three boys in the room. He was one of them. At Saint James, smoking cigarettes in a building brings suspension in the first instance and dismissal in the second. Smoking marijuana brings dismissal in the first instance. The next morning, the dean of students and I questioned each boy in turn. The first two responded predictably:

"Were you smoking?"

"Yes."

"What were you smoking?"

"Tobacco."

"What else were you smoking?"

"Nothing."

"Were you smoking marijuana?"

"No, I swear to God, I wasn't; you can ask the others."

And then we asked him:

"Were you smoking?"

"Yes."

"What were you smoking?"

"Tobacco."

"What else were you smoking?"

"Marijuana."

The dean and I were astounded. Never had we heard the truth about marijuana use from someone caught smoking it. After all, part of the decision to smoke marijuana is to lie about it; it's against the law, and it gets you dismissed from school. We were humbled by the integrity and courage we had just witnessed. When I asked him why he told the truth, he answered that he had to.

"I called my mom after I got caught, and I told her what had happened. She said to tell the truth and that you would expel me." "But surely you knew that you could get away with a suspension if you lied?" "Yes, but it wouldn't have been the same." "What do you mean?" "It wouldn't have felt the same if I had lied to you; it would have been different." "Where is your mother now?" "She's driving up to get me. She told me to pack my things."

During my time as headmaster, I have worked with many students and, thus, with many parents in difficult and challenging situations. I have become convinced that every situation, no matter how challenging, provides an occasion for us to teach and learn the right lessons.

That is what his mother did. She seized the occasion of her son's mistakes to teach him the right lessons: to tell the truth, to accept the consequences of his actions, and to restore the relationships that he had damaged. Disappointed as she was, she must have been tempted to teach him the wrong, more usual lessons: to lie and cover it up, to plead a false excuse. He had the usual opportunities: he could have blamed his friends, or even his Attention Deficit Disorder, but he did not. Encouraged by his parents, he told the truth, learning and growing because he did. The trajectory again was good.

Impressed by his response, I commended him to a nearby boarding school from which he subsequently graduated. The school is an athletic rival, so he played against us in soccer and lacrosse as brilliantly as he had played for us. Two years later, a student who had come to Saint James after him asked me why a leading player from the "rival" team had come over to hug me after a lacrosse game. "We are friends," I said.

His mother still sends me a birthday card every year full of his news. She is very proud of him.

A Letter to Supporters
Concerning Annual Giving

Dear Supporters of Saint James,

I thought about using the usual list of constituencies as I addressed you, "alumni, parents, parents of alumni and friends," but then it occurred to me that such a list is incomplete, as there are also grandparents, aunts and uncles, widows of alumni and perhaps most notably faculty and staff who have long set an example of loyalty and generosity in their giving to Saint James School. This past year, for example, every faculty and staff member made a gift to the Annual Fund. I should also note that every parent also gave. For those of you who give from a distance, this devotion and enthusiasm from those who know us best should be an encouragement. The term "friend" therefore is perhaps the best term for everybody, but you are more than friends, you are the friends who support us, remember us, and give to us when there are so many other worthy recipients of your treasure. I write then to you who are our supporters, all of you who for your own reasons and because of your own goodness step forward to sustain and build this school.

As I often explain to applicants and their parents when they first visit us, Saint James is unique in comparison to other schools, and we are unique in several ways. Academically, we provide a unique combination of strong preparation for college with a close and supportive environment; extracurricularly, we provide a full program in athletics and the arts, but also maintain a smaller, more involved enrollment; and morally, spiritually if you will, we still seek to encourage a personal growth in our students towards leadership and service which is distinctly our own. When I am asked to compare us to other schools, I find this very difficult. The schools we are like academically tend to be much larger than we are, and they also maintain a student culture on their campuses which is less focused academically, athletically, extracurricularly and spiritually. In their pursuit of excellence, they encourage their students to specialize early, to be more self-focused, and they tend to treat them like college undergraduates.

As you know, in our pursuit of excellence, we do not do this. In chapel and in the refectory, we gather as a school; we follow a core curriculum; we insist on athletic and extracurricular participation; and we challenge and nurture our students to encourage their spiritual growth.

There is something wonderful about the pattern of the day at Saint James, the way we journey through our day together. For me, the points of transition are particularly inspiring, as they are the commas in our sentence, bursts of energy and opportunities for fellowship in the regular pattern of our common life. I like the beginning of the day on campus when students walk through the mist in their blazers to chapel, the way they file out of chapel, row by row, youngest first; the mass migration to lunch as we come together in the new refectory; the mad dash to dorm rooms and locker rooms before sports; the return of teams from the playing fields, laughing and talking on their way to the showers; gathering again for dinner, chatting with friends as they wait to enter the dining hall; the shift out of blazers into comfortable clothes for evening study hall; the crowd in Kemp Hall before check in, sixth formers lingering just a little longer, savoring their last privilege in a long and busy day.

What a wonderful place you have built for us here, what a wonderful day you have given us, and what a tremendous gift of community and opportunity you make available so generously to each generation of students. We need your support, and we are grateful for it.

Yours faithfully,

The Revd. Dr. D. Stuart Dunnan
The Headmaster, Saint James School

A Sermon
The Faith They Will Need,
Parent's Weekend

For God did not give us a spirit of cowardice, but rather a spirit
of power and of love and of self-discipline.
2 Timothy 1:7

HIS IS MY TENTH PARENTS' WEEKEND AT SAINT JAMES, and the pattern is a familiar one. Parents arrive to visit their children, to meet their teachers and each other, to hear them sing and to watch their games, to meet their friends, and to get a sense of the school where they live and learn at a remove from you. For some of you, this distance is considerable, halfway around the world; for others, the distance is quite short, just down the road. But for all of you, even for returning parents, parents of older siblings already graduated, and parents who are alumni yourselves, there is a natural and appropriate desire to be sure that your children are safe here, that all is well with them, and that the journey begun and continuing here is going well.

For your children, increasingly independent and resilient in their journey to adulthood, parental concern is usually an embarrassment, and they do their best to calm your fears; but their grudging attempts at damage control are sometimes less than convincing to parents looking for the bulk of the iceberg beneath that placid surface. Thus, to the nervous parent, "don't worry, I'll fix my grades" sounds like a future without college; "it's just a cold" sounds like pneumonia; "it's just a sprain" sounds like a multiple fracture; and "we're just friends" sounds like an elopement.

And now there is something else to worry about. The terrorist attacks of September 11 have raised new, much more substantial fears. Will we go to war? And what will this war be like? Will we be attacked again? Where? How? Will our students and your children fight in this war? And even if they do not fight, what consequences will they suffer?

There is a fine line between worry and fear, and parents of teenagers today often hover on the brink of it. In one way, the events of last month help because they have given us a new perspective. The things that worried us before—what grade on the test, what result in the game, what college on the list—these things should seem to us less important; not unimportant, mind you, but more appropriately important. As I told the football team after they lost a hard-fought game to Sidwell Friends in an otherwise successful season, let us remember to pray for those who are suffering much more than we are.

But there are many ways in which these startling changes to our world threaten to bring us over the line. I had a sense of this on the day when we saw those horrifying pictures on television and heard the rumors spread by our newscasters. How many attacks were there? How many casualties? What about family and friends in Washington? in New York? or even just traveling? The phones started ringing, and messages flooded through the internet, as parents reached over the lines to hold their children, to assure them that they were safe, and to assure themselves that all was well.

And meanwhile, we went to school. As the crowd gathered to watch the spectacle on television in Kemp Hall during that first free period, I noticed a girl doing her homework as she watched. When I went to check on a student whose mother works in the Pentagon, he was working in his room. When I pulled another from class to check if her father, who is a Navy officer, also worked in the Pentagon, she told me that he worked in the Navy Yard and went back to class. Remarkably, we were untouched directly. Though our thoughts flew to the chairman of our board whose office was on the ninety-second floor of the second tower of the World Trade Center. Fortunately, he was traveling in Chicago, and he called to tell us so, but tragically he lost some 90 of his colleagues.

And we came back here. We came back to this chapel, all of us: staff, faculty, and students together. The liturgy formed itself. Father Gahan picked the readings and led us in prayer for our country. We sang the school hymn, the words of which took on a new meaning: "Oh God our help in ages past, our hope for years to come, our shelter from the stormy blast, and our eternal home." Our voice teacher, Mr. Rotz, sang "A Simple Song" from Leonard Bernstein's Mass: "Sing God a simple song, make it up as you go along, sing like you like to sing; God loves all simple things, for God is the simplest of all." And I spoke.

And what could I say but that we were safe, that things would not be as bad as they appeared at first, that America is a great power with a great presence in the world which produces enemies, that God is good, and that sometimes people are not?

And then the good people came forward, and the news began to change. Shocking images of burning and imploding skyscrapers were soon replaced by countless tales of devotion and of heroism, of firefighters and rescue workers offering their lives bravely to save others, of strangers helping strangers to escape, of doomed passengers on a hijacked jet overpowering their hijackers to save others on the ground.

Like the proverbial pebble thrown into the water, this act of hate and violence has been cushioned wonderfully by responding circles of love in the fabric of our society: in New York, which was before the most anonymous of cities, doctors and nurses rushed to hospitals to offer aid, people in neighborhoods unaffected waited in long lines to give blood as if it were a sale at Macy's. The whole country, and indeed the world, responded with real empathy and immediate support. Locally, strangers became neighbors, and neighbors became friends; nationally, political opponents praised each other openly and helped each other to do their jobs effectively; internationally, old allies rushed to our side, and old enemies became new friends.

And gone is this notion that religion is a merely private matter; it is corporate as well. Suddenly there is a new awareness that your religion matters to me. Negatively, if what another believes encourages that person to kill me, then I have the right to respond with what I believe to be right. Positively, if what we believe separately encourages us to bridge our differences and to live in peace and in love with one another, then we have a need to celebrate these good values which all our faiths would teach us and to embrace and strengthen that common conviction of goodness which unites us and preserves our commonwealth.

A relativist morality is a false luxury of peace and prosperity. Times of challenge and of hardship require moral absolutes. Let me state a few: It is good to offer oneself, even one's own life to help or indeed save another; It is good to defend the weak, to serve justice, and to preserve peace; To save oneself at the expense of another, or worse, to refuse to suffer hardship at the expense of another is morally weak and cowardly; To hate another for any reason, to be animated by hate, lost to hate, to seek revenge or to wish to brutalize because of hate can only be understood as evil.

The readings assigned for this Sunday remind us of these absolutes, and they remind us of the sacrifice they require, for scripture speaks to us from many times of challenge and from many places of hardship in our past of the steadfast purpose of God and of the faith which He requires.

In our reading from the Old Testament, the prophet Habakkuk speaks to his people in anticipation of the Babylonian invasion: "Look at the nations, and see! Be astonished! Be astounded! For a work is being done in your days that you would not believe if you were told. . . . Their horses are swifter than leopards, more menacing than wolves at dusk; their horses charge. Their horsemen come from far away; they fly like an eagle swift to devour. They all come for violence, with faces pressing forward; they gather captives like sand. At kings they scoff, and of rulers they make sport. They laugh at every fortress, and heap up earth to take it. Then they sweep by like the wind; they transgress and become guilty . . ." (Habakkuk 1:5 ff.)

But notice his warning to Judah not to make the same mistake themselves, to remember who they are, and more importantly whose they are, and to act in faith accordingly: "Look at the proud! Their spirit is not right in them, but the righteous live by their faith." (2:4)

And so also the psalmist reminds us: "The wicked draw their sword and bend their bow to strike down the poor and needy, to slaughter those who are upright in their ways. Their sword shall go through their own heart, and their bow shall be broken. The little that the righteous has is better than great riches of the wicked. For the power of the wicked shall be broken, but the Lord upholds the righteous." (Ps. 37:15–18)

And so in the passage from his second epistle to Timothy, St. Paul, who is in prison and expecting execution, writes to his followers exhorting them to be brave, not brave to triumph, but brave to be good: "Hold to the standard of sound teaching that you have heard from me, in the faith and love that are in Christ Jesus. Guard the good treasure entrusted to you, with the help of the Holy Spirit living in us." (2:14)

Our common tradition in the West as Christians, Jews, and Muslims reminds us that faith requires goodness and that goodness requires faith; the two are inseparable. To seek power or wealth or glory for their own sake is to forget our faith and to act against God's purpose; to serve the cause of peace and to offer ourselves to our neighbor is to keep our faith and to serve God's purpose. And the result of faith is power, not our power, but God's power. This is what Jesus meant when he said to his apostles, "If you had faith the size of a mustard seed, you could say to this mulberry tree, 'Be uprooted and planted in the sea,' and it would obey you." (Luke 17:6) If we had faith in God's great purpose and had the courage to play our part in His purpose, then the consequence would be huge.

Indeed, the best synonym for faith is courage, and courage is what these times (as all times) require: the courage to be good as God defines the good and reveals His good to us. And this means the courage to be generous in the face of greed, kind in the face of hatred, understanding in the face of prejudice, resilient in the face of hardship, and strong in the face of evil.

The truth is that the world your children face has not changed as much as we had fooled ourselves into believing, not because God does not will it to change, but because we often lack the faith to respond with the courage which His will for change requires. The challenge then which your children will face is the same challenge which we now face ourselves, and indeed the same challenge which the saints have faced before us: the challenge to be faithful in order to be good.

And so the smaller challenges your children face at Saint James will be good for them, because these challenges will give them the tools they will need for life, not life as we want it to be, or indeed pretend it to be, but life as it is. Working hard for the test, playing hard for the team, learning to be a true friend and a real leader, all of these challenges with all the pain they bring with them will equip your children for the greater challenges ahead. For it is through these challenges that they will gain that true "spirit of power and of love and of self-discipline" which St. Paul writes about and that empowering faith which Our Lord commends to us: the faith they will need to move the mountains of selfishness, hate, and prejudice which block the way of God ahead.

Amen.

A Sermon
Preached at All Saints Parish,
Chevy Chase

"Two men went up to the temple to pray . . ."
Luke 18:10

eing a headmaster, particularly the headmaster of a boarding school, and having therefore the care of young people, I find that I often hear the parables of Jesus in a different way than I did before I had this role. Specifically, when Jesus tries to teach us about our right relationship with God, I find that I have a great deal more understanding and sympathy for God's desire in that relationship with us than I had before.

Now this will come as no surprise to my students who cast me in the role of God quite often and think of me as sometimes confusing myself with God as I rule over their lives and determine their futures. But casting me in this role, they often adopt in fact a false understanding of how I view my role or indeed what I want from them as headmaster.

Parents of teenagers are obviously in a similar position, indeed a more powerful one, for in the eyes of their children, they assume the role of God, dispensing blessing and judgment and determining the very quality of their lives: "By my divine power, I give you these car keys, this car even, this stereo, this computer, this cell phone, this cash for your amusement. I allow you this freedom; I permit you these friendships; I tolerate these poor grades from you and assume these poor behaviors; I choose to believe you when I know that you are lying; I agree to blame the other when I know that you are at fault; I witness your victories and delight in your boasting; I ignore your failures and suffer your whining; I care for your every need and bend to your every mood. Unless by my divine power, I choose not to give you the keys, the car, the stereo, the computer, the cell phone, the cash for your date. I choose not to allow your freedom or permit your friendships; I condemn your poor grades as unworthy of you and reject your poor behavior as destructive and demeaning; I know that you are lying, and I do not agree to blame the other for what you in fact have done; I ignore your victories and reject your boasting as vain and self-serving; I notice your failures and call them to your attention constantly; I forget your needs and refuse to be your servant."

At least, so it would appear to your children. But parents of teenagers and teenagers in healthy relationships with their parents know that this is a false view of the parental role, just as students of mine who settle into the school and come to know me as a priest and a person also know that theirs was a false view of the headmaster's role, as I am not just the dispenser of judgment, punishment, and praise. I am also the supporter, counselor, protector, teacher, and friend.

In fact, I cherish that wonderful moment of enlightenment that comes in my relationship with a student when he or she first realizes that Father Dunnan is not quite what he or she thought I was, and this comes when that student turns to me for help, not for punishment or praise, mind you, but for help: "Father, my girlfriend just dumped me and I really loved her, what can I do? My teacher hates me. We lost the game, because of me. The college I wanted rejected me. My friend needs me, but I can't help. My roommate is driving me nuts. Why wasn't I invited? My parents don't understand me. My dad and my mom are breaking up."

And these moments are multiple, of course, and the conversations that come with them quite holy. Each time a student opens his or her heart and turns to me for help, the relationship between us deepens. By listening to that student and seeking to understand that student, by stopping to be with that student and giving that student my full attention and my time, I have offered a pause from the troubles of this life, perhaps a new perspective, and the real assurance of my love. The headmaster, one who sits in authority over you and cannot stray from the truth even for your sake, that one roots for you, cares about you, and wants to sit with you and listen.

Now what I know in relationship to my students over four to five years, parents know in relationship to their children, God willing, for many decades. It just happens that I work with adolescents, and thus live with their children during a time in their development when they are trying to break away from their parents emotionally and therefore need, at times, to turn to someone else. Nonetheless, I am sure that all of you who are or have been parents of teenagers know exactly what I am talking about, the important moments for growth in relationship to your children come in those conversations when they turn to you, not to demand some right or beseech some gift, or even to avoid some punishment, but when they turn to you for help.

Those of you who are parents of small children have these conversations 100 times a day. Cherish them; they begin to peter out. As children grow older, they grow more independent, and that is as it should be, but adolescence is a particularly poignant time, because they are not really independent yet, they want to be, they need to be, but you still direct and sustain their lives. And so the hard part is that you are still close enough to suffer with them and to want to protect them, and they will not always let you. To quote my professor in pastoral care in seminary, "they have to bounce."

Isn't this what Jesus is saying about God in relationship to us? And isn't this why he encourages us to pray to God as our parent? Remember how he taught us to pray. "You pray like this: 'Our Father. . .' "

And isn't this just the problem that he seeks to reveal to us with his parable? When it comes to our relationship to the Father in prayer, we are acting like a bunch of adolescents, keeping our Father at a distance, failing to turn to Him in our need, rather boasting to Him falsely, begging from Him, avoiding Him, using Him, trying even to fool Him when we know that we can't.

Like me in relationship to my students and like the parent in relationship to the teenager, God is right here with us, close to us, directing and sustaining our lives. He is ready to help us. He knows us and cares for us, and offers for us, always, the opportunity to come and to talk with Him, to be ourselves with Him, to pause with Him from the worries of our lives, to gain His fresh perspective, and to know that we are loved.

This parable in which Our Lord compares the vain Pharisee who boasts of his righteousness before God to the repentant tax collector who confesses his sins is indeed a parable about humility: "for all who exalt themselves will be humbled, (and) all who humble themselves will be exalted." But it is ultimately a parable about prayer. Unless we can live through our adolescence in relationship to the Father, we will never grow into relationship with Him and thus never grow into His purpose with our lives. As long as we avoid God, He will wait for us; as long as we ignore him, He will love us; but we will always fear Him, resent Him, avoid Him, never love Him back.

It is only then when we turn to God as our parent in prayer and offer to Him our needs honestly and humbly that we will know Him as He really is and wants to be in relationship to us. He is more than father and even more than mother to us; He is Love for us itself, the one true love which is best and always for us.

And I bet those of us who care or who have cared for teenagers closely know exactly how God feels about us, as He listens to our requests for things and our demands for rights and boasts of triumphs, as he watches us fail without His help and waits to hear the truth He knows with all the pain that He would share with us. He waits for us to come to Him for help, and to learn in our need that He loves us.

Amen.

A Sermon
At the Alumni Eucharist

All of you, have unity of spirit, sympathy, love for one another, a
tender heart, and a humble mind.
1 Peter 3:8

UST RECENTLY, I asked a student who will be leaving Saint James at the end of the year what he thought he had learned with us. Knowing him well, I was interested in his answer, and I think that I was expecting him to say something like "I learned how to work hard here," or "I learned to tell the truth," or "to be kind." At least, I was hoping he would say something like that.

His answer surprised me: "I learned how to get along with people from different backgrounds and different countries."

His answer reminded me of a comment that Bishop Ihloff once made to me during a picnic lunch in front of Claggett after a confirmation service. Sitting on the front porch and watching the faculty and students interact on the central circle in front of us, he turned to me and said, "This is a vision of heaven, you know." Surprised, I asked him what he meant. "Look at them," he said, "you've got all types of people out there, all the races of the world in fact, and nobody notices. Let's hope they stay that way."

Peter Relic, who served for the last ten years or so as president of the National Association of Independent Schools, used to give a speech in which he exhorted the assembled school heads to welcome the world onto our campuses and to educate our students as broadly as possible, to teach them about non-Western as well as Western culture and history, to expand the traditional core of our curricula beyond America and the English-speaking world, beyond

166

the Western corpus to other voices and other traditions alive and vital in the world today.

Newly returned from England and steeped in the Western corpus, I chuckled to myself, sneered inwardly at the "politically correct" culture of the NAIS establishment, and dismissed his appeal as impractical and naive. He used to tell a particularly implausible story about a beggar selling pencils at the Taj Mahal who could hawk his wares in five languages, and was therefore supposedly better educated than our students. Later, he told the same story about a taxi driver in New York City . . .

But after I had settled in, I soon faced some realities. First, because of our proximity to Washington and because of a tradition of international students begun by Father Owens after the Second World War, Saint James boasted a healthy compliment of international students. In fact, the year I arrived, we had students from Thailand, Hong Kong, South Korea, Mexico, Saudi Arabia, and Japan. Interestingly, many of these students had found out about us in just the same way that the American students had: word of mouth. Family members, neighbors, colleagues had recommended Saint James to them because of the good experience of their own children, just as they would in Maryland, Pennsylvania or South Carolina.

Over the years, the good word has spread. Excluding American students whose families live abroad, by my count, the present student body boasts members from 15 different countries: Canada, Nigeria, Ivory Coast, Uganda, Taiwan, China, Thailand, Korea, Japan, Germany, Poland, the Czech Republic, Kazakhstan, the Ukraine, and Russia. In fact, Saint James's reputation abroad is so strong that we can enroll students whose English is sufficiently proficient to study in English with only minimal ESL support outside the classroom.

And because America is itself a country of immigrants, our American students are hardly homogeneous either. Indeed, many of our American students come from immigrant families where English is not their first language, but rather languages like Hindi, Urdu, Korean, Spanish, and Russian. In fact, because of the significant role of immigrant doctors in our local medical community, our Hagerstown students are probably the most diverse of all.

Further, because of these differences in the ethnic and cultural background of our students, we are religiously diverse as well. Indeed, I often remark to the students that we have every major religion in the world represented in the student body: all the major Christian confessions, Jews, Muslims, Buddhists, and

Hindus. Recently, Jae-Woo Lee read his senior essay in Chapel in which he spoke of his five-year journey as a Buddhist at Saint James. When he arrived as a second former, he was struck by our differences, and he was stuck on our differences. But then, inspired as he was by the "gentle persuasion" (as he put it) of his headmaster, he joined the choir, and he has discovered in himself a real talent for singing, a real joy in singing, and a new appreciation for the liturgical and choral tradition which is the glory of Anglicanism, though he is still, as he proclaimed with pride in his essay, very much a Buddhist. Indeed, I would say that he is even more of a Buddhist than he was before, no longer the defiant teenager with an attitude, but now a more humble disciple of the "inner way."

Listening to Jae-Woo read his essay, in excellent English, by the way, I thought of several Jewish students who have also sung in the choir. I thought of a Muslim student who was one of our best ushers, and a Hindu student who surprised me one commencement when he presented himself in the sacristy as the crucifer. "Is this all right with your religion?" I asked. "Sure, Father," he answered, "we are into images too." His parents proudly photographed him, as he processed triumphantly by.

Academically, our English and history curricula have adjusted to our smaller world as well. Fourth form students take a course in non-Western history, which we call developing nations, and sixth form English students study non-Western literature after a year of British and then American literature. In the French and Spanish programs, students now read literature by African, as well as Central and South American writers. Even in my A.P. European History class, I find myself spending much more time on Balkan and Central European History, as well as the impact of European imperialism on non-Western cultures and societies. I remember describing the Burma campaign in a class on World War II, only to discover that one of my students knew more about it than I did, because his grandfather had fought for the British Empire in that campaign as an officer in the Indian army.

So despite initial appearances, Saint James is in fact quite remarkable for its racial, cultural, national, and religious diversity, and our curriculum reflects this diversity much more than it did ten years ago. However, what is perhaps most interesting about our diversity, and certainly most encouraging, is just what Bishop Ihloff noticed during that picnic: our reaction to our diversity, or rather our lack of reaction. For in truth, we do not recognize just how diverse we are; it usually takes someone from outside our community to notice it and to point it out to us. And the reason we do not recognize our diversity is because we are a community. Because we are a community, we relate to each other as friends, not as strangers; and because we are a community dedicated to learning, we join in our common task as teachers and students together, studying the world as it is, learning from each other, and thus benefiting as we do from each other's distinct background and experience.

In my fifth year as headmaster, Dr. Newman and Ms. Pollock organized a series of student and faculty seminars focusing on ethical issues pertinent to our time. As Director of the National Association, Peter Relic came out to join us and to see what we were doing. After his day at school, he came into my office ecstatic, and I was frankly surprised by the fervor of his reaction. "Stuart," he said, "you have the most wonderful school." "Really, Peter, why?" "This is the world, you have here." "What do you mean?" "Well, I just came from a discussion group on global warming in which a student from Thailand and a student from Nigeria were talking about the impact of first world policies upon their respective countries, and everybody was interested. It was amazing." "Oh," I thought, "I guess I did what he wanted after all."

The truth, of course, is that I had done nothing, really; I had just reacted to the changing world around us. Ours is a good and safe place, and we happen to be next to the seat of government of the world's greatest superpower, and for these two reasons, the world has come to us. And coming to us, students with different cultural and national backgrounds have come not just to learn about our English-speaking culture and American greatness, but to teach us about their cultures, their faiths, and their national struggles as well. We have, therefore, all of us learned from each other, which is just what God intends.

In the passage appointed for today from St. John's Gospel, Jesus speaks of himself as "the true vine" and of the Father as "the vinegrower." We are the branches. (John 15:1–8) Traditionally, Christians have tended to feel pretty smug about this passage, as it appears to suggest that we have an exclusive and favored relationship with God, making us better than other people. Jesus's point, of course, is quite the opposite.

If we think of Jesus as St. John presents him, as the revealer of the divine purpose or the will of God which is love, then we can appreciate that what he is saying to us is that he can connect us to this purpose, just as a vine connects the branches to the soil which nourishes them. The proof of our connection is the fruit that we bear: acts and words which serve God's will. "Those who abide in me and I in them bear much fruit, because apart from me you can do nothing." Thus, he is not telling us that we are better than everybody, because we believe in him, but rather that we are called by him to enter into a more faithful relationship with the Father which should serve the Father's will.

Notice, therefore, what he does not say. He does not say, "I am the vine, and you are the branch." He says, "You are the branches." There are many of us, not just one. Also, he does not say "you are the vine, and I am the branch." Ours is not to use Christ for our service, but rather the other way around. We are to be used by Christ for His service.

Back in 1862, Dr. Kerfoot looked at Saint James and compared it to the world around him, a country wracked by civil war. Looking to this society and at the way his southern students and northern faculty were able to live and learn together, he was encouraged, even inspired: "How the College and its government will bear itself amid the strifes of the times, the declarations made here a year ago, and the independent, prudent, impartial accomplishment since, sufficiently show–that here, in harmony, on an equality, and amid some fair measure of efficient working, young men may yet meet and live together, to learn how personal affections and courtesy ought to and may smooth down the ill-tempers and distrust that ought never to have arisen."[1]

So we in our generation can look to the society we know at Saint James and compare it to the world, not just America any more, but the whole world, divided as it is by religious and ethnic strife, misdirected as it is by materialistic selfishness, mutual ignorance, increasing distrust, and brutal, vicious violence. Like Kerfoot in his time, we too in our time can look to the world and lose heart, or we can look to Saint James and take heart.

Let us listen then to the words of St. Peter and make them our rule of life: "All of you, have unity of spirit, sympathy, love for one another, a tender heart, and a humble mind." Let us love one another, learn from each other, and change the world together, humbly, tenderly, sympathetically, spiritually, just as God intends. Somebody has to, and God appears to have given us the grace to do it.

This then is what God requires of us, all of us, Christian, Jew, Muslim, Buddhist, Hindu, Catholic, Protestant, European, African, American, black, brown, white, rich, poor, northern, southern, city, country, however we can be different. We must lose our labels to live in love as friends, and this we

---

[1] Harrison, *Life of Kerfoot*, vol. I, p. 231.

must do, for we are, all of us, branches of the same vine, rooted in the same soil, and called to bear the same good fruit, reflecting the good purpose of the Creator of us all.

So look around you, especially those who are leaving and those who are returning to this place which you once left. Stop and remember the kind of society which exists here, the fellowship of it. No place is perfect, and certainly no school is perfect; but in this particular regard, Saint James is indeed quite different. The Bishop was right; Peter Relic was right: in the many good ways in which we are able to forget our differences here and to learn and grow together, God has granted us a vision, a vision of His heaven. Let us be mindful of this, and let us bring His heaven to His earth.

Amen.

ABOUT THE AUTHOR

APPOINTED HEADMASTER OF SAINT JAMES SCHOOL in June of 1992 when he was only 33 years old, the Revd. Dr. D. Stuart Dunnan has presided over a remarkable revival of this historic Episcopal boarding school in Western Maryland. A teacher and chaplain at both the school and university levels before he came to Saint James, he is one of the few Episcopal priests still serving as the head of a secondary school in the United States. He is also one of a decreasing number of independent school heads to serve the same school for more than five years, in his case, ten and counting.

Born and raised in Washington, D.C., Father Dunnan holds a bachelor's and a master's degree in history from Harvard University and a masters and a doctoral degree in theology from Oxford University in England. As an educator and preacher, he is particularly interested in the moral and spiritual formation of teenagers, and thus eager to "encourage their goodness" and to "challenge their selfishness" within the context of their actual lives.

At a time when many Episcopal schools have developed away from their church identities, some boarding schools have become day schools, and most secondary schools have grown larger, Father Dunnan has strengthened the church identity of Saint James, restored its boarding program, and preserved its smaller size, while also increasing its diversity and improving the quality of its academic and extracurricular programs. In doing this, he has developed a strong apology for Episcopal schools, for boarding schools, and for smaller, more focused secondary school communities. In all three ways, his argument is distinct, and he provides a uniquely encouraging perspective for secondary school educators and for parents of teenagers in America today.